"In *Man to Man*, my dear friend and American hero, LTG William 'Jerry' Boykin, has clearly laid out God's master plan for men and our crucial role in American culture. The future of our nation depends on reestablishing Godly manhood and this book is the strategy to get us there. Get it for yourself, the men with whom you keep company, and tell your church about it."

—Oliver L. North,
bestselling author of *The Rifleman*

"Young men aspire to it. Women admire them. A real man. We all understand that when men get it right, everyone wins—men, women, children. But when a man gets it wrong, everyone hurts. Badly. It's not easy being a real man in a culture where the definition of masculinity is in a moral free fall. In a day of extremism surrounding gender issues, *Man to Man* offers a refreshing and respectful balance in pointing the way to real manhood. Every man needs a manly mentor to show him the path to real manhood. Jerry Boykin is such a man. His military resume over a lifetime in Special Operations speaks for itself—one tough hombre! There is more. In this book you will go beyond the warrior's resume. You will pull the curtain back to find the warm, relational heart of a family man. Boykin gives valuable insight into five key elements of real manhood. We all need to take it to heart."

—Stu Weber, pastor and author

"*Man to Man* is a timely book that cuts straight to the foundations of masculinity. This book is a practical guide to real masculinity and is full of personal accounts and war stories that make the author's points while keeping the reader glued to the book."

—Honorable Ken Blackwell,
former US Ambassador UN Human Rights
Commission, former mayor of Cincinnati

"*Man to Man* is a refreshing and timely look at masculinity at a time when men are confused as to how the term applies in their lives. With over thirty-six years in the U.S. Army, serving in the Green Berets, Rangers, and Delta Force, LTG(R) Boykin has served with real men and this book reflects what he has learned about what real masculinity is according to God's design."

—Bishop Larry Jackson,
Bethel Outreach International Church

MAN TO MAN

REDISCOVERING MASCULINITY
IN A CHALLENGING WORLD

LTG (Ret.) WILLIAM G. BOYKIN
WITH LELA GILBERT

FIDELIS
BOOKS

A FIDELIS BOOKS BOOK
An Imprint of Post Hill Press
ISBN: 978-1-64293-368-0
ISBN (eBook): 978-1-64293-369-7

Man to Man:
Rediscovering Masculinity in a Challenging World
© 2020 by LTG (Ret.) William G. Boykin
All Rights Reserved

Scripture used in this book comes from:
NIV—THE HOLY BIBLE, NEW INTERNATIONAL VERSION®, NIV®
Copyright © 1973, 1978, 1984, 2011 by Biblica, Inc.® Used by permission. All
rights reserved worldwide.
KJV—The King James Version of the Bible is public domain in the United States.
NKJV—New King James Version®. Copyright © 1982 by Thomas Nelson. Used
by permission. All rights reserved.
NASB—NEW AMERICAN STANDARD BIBLE®, Copyright © 1960, 1962,
1963, 1968, 1971, 1972, 1973, 1975, 1977, 1995 by The Lockman Foundation.
Used by permission.

Dr. Kenyn Cureton as a research contributor and provided the
Discussion Questions for each chapter

Post Hill Press
New York • Nashville
posthillpress.com

Published in the United States of America

Also by LTG (Ret.) William G. Boykin

*Never Surrender: A Soldier's Journey to the
Crossroads of Faith and Freedom*
The Coalition: A Novel
*The Warrior Soul: Five Powerful Principles
to Make You a Stronger Man of God*
Kiloton Threat: A Novel
Danger Close: A Novel

To my dad, Gerald Boykin, and my wife, Ashley,
both of whom taught me how to be a man.

CONTENTS

FOREWORD

Men who fear God, not people, can change the world! As a veteran of the Marine Corps, former law enforcement officer, and policy maker on the state and now national level for years, and as the president of Family Research Council, I can tell you with certainty America's future will not be decided by what happens in Washington, D.C., or even in your state capitol—it will be decided by what happens in homes all across America, including yours. God-fearing men who love their wives, invest in their children, and embrace their role as the spiritual leaders of their homes can turn America around.

Those are not just words. I believe that. So much so that it has become my life's focus. I have never been more excited in my adult life, about the future of this country, than right now. Yes, there are many bad things happening in our culture; the challenges are almost indescribable. I never thought I would see some of the moral insanity I see today. Yet, I am also seeing good things, opportunities God has given to the church in this moment, that I never thought I would see. It is up to men, who know God, to become what He has designed us to be, so we can be used by Him, to change the world around us. Consequently, I believe the greatest need in America today is for men to stand courageous and fearlessly follow God, like the author of this book, Family Research Council Executive Vice President, General Jerry Boykin.

General Boykin spent over thirty-six years in the United States Army. He is a man's man. His last duty was at the Pentagon as the deputy undersecretary of defense for intelligence. He has played a role in almost every recent major American military operation over the last four decades, serving in Grenada, Somalia, and Iraq. From 1978–1993 he was assigned in various capacities to Delta Force. Not only was he a founding member of the Delta Force, he has also led Green Berets and other special operations units many times. Among his many successful operations was one in October of 1983—the beginning of the end of the Soviet Communist regime. A major at the time, General Boykin worked as an operations officer during Operation Urgent Fury in Grenada. During a dawn assault to free government officials, held by the Marxist People's Revolutionary Army, he was shot in the arm with a fifty-caliber round, splitting his bone completely in two. He was told he would never use his arm again, but God had the final say and today you would never even know he was injured. His citations for valor are too numerous to list.

God has had His hand on this man from start to finish and He is not finished with him yet. General Boykin is an author, an ordained minister, a professor, and a decorated war hero for which he has my most profound respect and admiration. His courage and commitment to the truth extend beyond the physical field of battle. He not only has been willing to lay down his life for his country, he has been willing to lay down his life for his Lord and Savior, Jesus Christ, and his reputation to serve Him. General Boykin will not shut up; he will not back up; he will not give up. He is a hero among heroes. He is the kind of man I want by my side in the spiritual war that is raging in America today. I believe as the apostle Paul relays to us, in the orders from our heavenly Commander In Chief, that we are to honor those who are deserving of honor. As this man has stood and continues to stand, I certainly honor him, I'm grateful for him, and I am honored to provide this forward and pleased to recommend his book, *Man to Man*.

My prayer is you will fear God above all and fearlessly fulfil His plans and purposes for your life as a man. General Boykin's book is filled with biblical and experiential wisdom to help, outlining five biblical roles and responsibilities of every God-honoring man. May you become the faithful provider, inspiring instructor, fearless defender, trustworthy mentor, and the godly chaplain God has called you to be in your family, church, and community.

—Tony Perkins, president of Family Research Council

CECIL—WHAT A MAN IS SUPPOSED TO BE

Before you read on about men, godly masculinity, and what roles a man is meant to play, I want to introduce you to a man—a real *man*—who I knew very well. His name was Cecil.

Growing up on a tobacco farm, Cecil was one of ten children. He had relatively little formal education. He was the youngest of the six boys in his family, so he stayed on the farm while four of his older brothers went off to fight during the Second World War. The only one of his brothers who did not enlist was the eldest. He had a family when the war started and was neither eligible for the draft nor acceptable for enlistment.

Cecil was raised in a home that believed in America, family, and God, as core values. They were poor by today's standards, but they always had food to eat and a roof over their heads. More importantly, they had each other, and their family was beloved by each of them.

Cecil turned seventeen in April of 1943. Only a few days after his birthday, he slipped away from the farm one afternoon and caught a ride with a local farmer into town. The reason for this foray was to pay a visit to the local U.S. Navy recruiting office. The recruiter was most accommodating in getting Cecil signed up for a three-year hitch and a trip to the European Theater. Why? There was no real question—Cecil loved America and he loved his family. With four brothers already deployed, Cecil wanted to do his part as an American and as the family member of proud patriots.

As the sun rose over the Normandy beaches on June 6th, 1944, Cecil was at the helm of a U.S. Navy LCVP landing craft (Higgins boat). He was delivering soldiers of the U.S. Army's First Infantry Division—The Big Red One—as the long-anticipated invasion of the continent of Europe finally unfolded.

As they approached the beach, Cecil and his fellow soldiers were in the line of sight of Nazi Germany's beach defenses. Fire from small arms, heavy machine guns, mortars, and myriad artillery blasted out of the concrete emplacements and fighting positions of the German lines. Cecil was duly warned by his concerned mother not to volunteer for anything. Sadly, he failed to heed her warning on that historic day, and as a result he would be the only one of the brothers wounded in WWII.

When Cecil awoke in the Portsmouth Naval Hospital in Virginia, he had only faint memories of the explosion that disabled his Higgins boat and killed or wounded several of the men. He was confused and a little delirious as he tried to recall all that happened over the past week, but most of it was shrouded in a fog of confusion with only short clips of reality coming back to him.

Cecil knew he was hit by enemy fire and knocked unconscious. But something else was seriously wrong and he couldn't yet determine exactly whether it was due to the sedatives he was given or not. Eventually, his attending physician entered the room with the bad news. Cecil was now blind in his left eye, and his sight would never return. It was the result of a direct hit on his boat by—what was most likely—a lucky shot with a German mortar round. Cecil would be given a medical discharge and deemed disabled by the Veterans Administration. Left with no other choice, Cecil accepted the discharge, and returned to his family's tobacco farm.

Two years after leaving the U.S. Navy, Cecil married his high school sweetheart and started a family. Since he hadn't completed high school, his opportunities were limited. So, he reverted to the one thing he had some knowledge of: farming. But his heart was still in service to his country. He missed the Navy and felt a sense of loss not being able to contribute to something bigger than himself—something that allowed him to be proud of his work.

Cecil wanted to serve in spite of his disability. It seemed impossible, but he wasn't ready to give up hope of putting on the military uniform once more. Finally, in 1948, the U.S. Army opened its ranks to disabled veterans who could still function. Any enlistee who joined under this program had to agree to attend one of several universities to become qualified in a particular skillset—usually having to do with electronics and communications. Cecil was ecstatic upon hearing this news. But, could he qualify? Had enthusiasm been the deciding factor, Cecil was a sure bet to be a soldier, but his eyesight was still in question.

The day of his entrance exam came quickly. Cecil experienced intense anxiety as he reported to the medical station, which was about forty miles from his hometown. He was about to face an exam that would, in his mind, determine his future and that of his family. His medical records told the doctors what they needed to know about his injuries from WWII; what was left to be determined was whether he could function adequately in the U.S. Army.

Thankfully, the outcome of his physical exam that day was exactly what Cecil hoped for. He was declared physically acceptable to serve in the electronics field, after completing the necessary training and education. Cecil was beyond pleased; in fact, he was a bit giddy as he explained to his wife, the mother of his six-month-old child, they were headed for Fort Bliss, Texas, to attend classes at Texas Western University of Mines in El Paso.

A week later Cecil raised his right hand for the second time in his life and swore to support and defend the U.S. Constitution. Cecil and his wife found a small apartment just outside Fort Bliss and Cecil became a college student—without ever having finished high school. All he wanted was opportunity and nothing more. Just opportunity. In 1948, the U.S. Army was giving him exactly that. He was determined to make the best of it because he loved America, just as he loved his family.

In June 1950, the North Korean army leader, Kim II Sung, crossed the thirty-eighth parallel into South Korea, initiating what came to be known as the Korean War. America quickly entered the conflict by sending troops who were already stationed in Japan. Landing in the southern port of Pusan, the American task force was called Task Force Smith, named after their commander Lieutenant Colonel Charles Smith. Cecil was once again a member of a military at war. Serving his country was exactly what Cecil wanted to be doing, especially with his nation involved in a conflict that threatened America's future, as well as her allies. Because, after all—besides loving his nation—he was convinced serving her was his responsibility.

The Korean War did not end as Cecil hoped. It was not the clear-cut victory for the United States WWII was. This war ended in a cease-fire armistice with no capitulation on either side. Also, for Cecil, the war was not the same as his previous experience because he was not deployed to the battlefront. Much to his dismay, he remained at Fort Bliss.

Nevertheless, service during the Korean War in any capacity qualified him as a Korean War era vet. After he completed his training at Fort Bliss, Cecil served the remainder of his enlistment. He then left the army to take a job with the U.S. Marine Corps as a civil servant. Once more, Cecil took an oath to serve, affirming his love for America and for his family. And the day would come in his life when he would also love God with all his heart.

For the next thirty-two years, Cecil served the nation as a U.S. Marine Corps civil servant and traveled globally with the marines, including a tour in Vietnam, 1967–1968. The 1968 Tet Offensive of the North Vietnamese occurred while he was there. His base, Da Nang, was a primary target of the enemy. While Cecil was not excited about being shot at again, he was certainly proud to be there with the marines as they fought against the brutality and repression of the Ho Chi Minh regime.

Eventually Cecil retired from civil service and decided to pursue his great passions: grandchildren, hunting, fishing, and baseball. But he never stopped loving America.

When the flag passed by during a parade, Cecil saluted. When the national anthem was played at the Babe Ruth League baseball games, he stood and placed his hat over his heart. Cecil belonged to the American Legion so he could be around other veterans. He also coached baseball for the local American Legion post. He was a patriot who was unashamed of his deep love and respect for the nation he faithfully served. America gave him opportunity, which was all he'd ever really wanted.

A "man's man" would be a good description of Cecil. He was what his generation expected a man to be—a courageous leader who loved the outdoors and all it provided: hunting, fishing, and sports.

He spent many hours teaching the skills of the outdoors to his children and grandchildren. Despite his blindness in one eye, Cecil was a crack shot who could put his buddies with two eyes to shame in the duck blind or the dove field. When it came to shooting a rifle, he was known as the "Rifleman" by his friends.

Several years after Cecil's children finished college and began their own careers and families, he brought home a twelve-year-old boy and announced to his wife that Shakeef would be living with them for a while. Cecil told his adult children to treat this boy like one of their brothers. As he did with his own sons, Cecil made Shakeef his constant companion, including trips to the movies, baseball games, and even to the regular breakfast meeting with his veteran buddies.

It wasn't long before Shakeef's race came up with some of Cecil's friends. Shakeef was black and the small southern town where Cecil lived still had a fair amount of racism within its society. Cecil had no intention of backing down from helping this boy who had no father in his home and needed an opportunity to succeed. Cecil's response when the matter was raised was simply, "Mind your own damn business." He was committed to the lad and determined to provide Shakeef with the same level of opportunity he had when he was that age.

Cecil kept Shakeef for well over a year and helped him become a good baseball player with the best equipment Cecil could buy him. He loved the boy and had a deep passion for seeing him progress in life. As far as Cecil was concerned, a boy growing up without a father was about the worst thing that could happen to a young fellow like

Shakeef. Here was an opportunity to make a difference in a boy's life and Cecil didn't hesitate to seize it.

Regardless of his lack of formal education, Cecil was a man of great wisdom, courage, and commitment to the things he valued. At age sixty-five, Cecil made the most important commitment of his life when he acknowledged Jesus Christ as the Lord of his life. Interestingly, before he accepted Christ as his Savior, Cecil was a fairly avid reader of the Bible. Consequently, he knew Scripture and could quote much of it, although he didn't have a solid understanding. Once he made the life-changing decision to follow Christ, Scripture took on new meaning and came alive for him. In fact, some would call Cecil a religious fanatic. It was as if he was trying to make up for all the time he wasted before deciding to follow Christ.

In his last couple of years, before he went to be with the Lord, Cecil spent much of his time in a hospital room. After visiting Cecil's room one day, the chaplain decided not to return. It turned out Cecil was trying to lead him to Christ. Cecil wanted to pray for the chaplain and was determined to help him find Jesus. The chaplain was having none of it and stopped visiting Cecil's room.

Cecil's faith in God became the centerpiece of his life.

Because of his great love for baseball, and his commitment to coaching the Babe Ruth League and the American Legion teams in his hometown, the people referred to him as "Mr. Baseball." Before he died, Cecil was honored by local officials when the high school baseball field was named after him. Today, baseball fans watch the high school team play on the Gerald Cecil Boykin Baseball Field in New Bern, North Carolina.

I know you probably saw that coming, but I enjoy telling my father's story just the same.

I grew up under the leadership and tutelage of a real man who taught me about respect for the flag, pride in being an American, and expecting only opportunity from this great nation. He was so proud of my brother and me because we chose to serve in the U.S. Army. My sister was married to an army officer as well, and my dad saw his dreams for his children fulfilled as we all served in some measure. It was important to him for us to carry on with the tradition of military service. I had no choice but to love America and to show that love by serving. If you were a male in the Boykin family and carried the family name, you were expected to serve. Two of my sons followed the tradition and joined the army. I am so proud of them.

The point here is being a man is not about education level, physical strength, annual salary, or good looks. Rather, it is about character and demonstrated values. I was blessed to be raised by a real man who taught me a great deal about life. A man who set a great example and who invested in me with his time and energy.

This book is not about Cecil, but I would not be writing it if it weren't for him and the influence he had on my life.

CHAPTER ONE

MAN AS THE PROVIDER

Being a great leader, provider, and protector is every man's mission. It doesn't matter how old you are, your vocation (single, married, priest, religious), or your career. If you're a man on this planet, God calls you to be a strong leader, provider, and protector. It has been my experience that when men understand what it means, and embrace it as their mission, life becomes much easier. In any situation, they know what their job is.

—Dr. Peter Kleponis, *Those Catholic Men*

But if any man does not provide for his own, and especially for those of his household, he has denied the faith and is worse than an unbeliever

—*1 Timothy 5:8 (NKJV)*

As you've read, my father Cecil Boykin was a man who knew what was important in life. And as long as he lived, he remained true to his personal values.

When his mother and father were no longer able to manage the farm Cecil grew up on, they were suddenly left with no place to live for their retirement.

Although they had ten children, only one of them came up with a solution for their dilemma—that man was my father. Cecil was far from wealthy and didn't have the option of taking money out of a savings account or cashing in some Wall Street investments. Instead, he used his disability pension to provide for his parents by building a small home for them, because Cecil's family had always lived in rented homes.

A couple of years after Cecil's parents moved into the new home, his youngest sister, Faye, and her husband also moved in with their parents because Faye's husband was disabled and bedridden. After both my grandparents died, my father sold that house to his nephew, Faye's son, who also grew up there. Cecil sold the home for far less than what it was worth as a way of supporting his sister and her invalid husband.

I find myself at times wondering how many of today's generation would feel the way Cecil did or do what he did. I even wonder if I would have made that sacrifice in the same situation.

There's a biblical mandate for us, as fathers and sons, to take care of our families—including our extended families—and also to look after others as needs arise.

Cecil's habit of providing for others wasn't limited to his immediate family. One day he got word his best friend had lost his home in a fire. At that time Cecil was struggling to pay his own bills. But that didn't stop him: he cut corners and scraped together whatever he could. And he gave his friend all the cash he could find.

I remember that day—as he handed the cash to his friend—because it looked like so much money to me at the time. I would guess it was no more than a hundred dollars in various denominations of bills, but to an eight-year-old it looked like a fortune. It left a powerful impression on me and just deepened my respect and admiration for him over the years.

Throughout my life my father exhibited many examples for me to follow concerning the responsibility a man has to care for those he loves and for those who are in need.

My father firmly believed it wasn't the U.S. government's responsibility to take care of his parents, his children, his friends, or his neighbors. In fact, in his view, it was his role as an American who loved his country to help provide for others as much as possible.

All Cecil Boykin ever wanted from his American homeland was opportunity. Everything else would come from his own hard work, self-reliance, and, when necessary, generosity.

What does being a "provider" have to do with me?

Maybe you're a little surprised the book you're holding in your hands is suggesting—right off the bat—that a man is intended to be a *Provider*.

You might be especially puzzled if you're a young, single man. Right now, you don't have a wife or children to worry about. Though you're interested in learning more about being a godly man, providing for others may not seem like it's something you need to know about.

Or maybe you're retired and you don't think being a provider is your responsibility anymore.

Or maybe you've been out of work for a while. You're frustrated because you haven't found a new job, and perhaps your wife is working and picking up the slack. Being a provider may not seem to be your job, but I contend it is. A man is meant to be a provider of much more than dollars and cents. And although eventually your wife and kids will be the primary beneficiaries of your provision, there are many other ways men can—and should—provide for others, even outside the family circle.

And it bears repeating a man is called to provide far more than money.

A man provides leadership.

A man provides direction, caution, and
advice to others.

A man provides emotional and spiritual support.

A man provides stability and order.

A man provides companionship and good company.

A man provides identity.

A man provides an example.

All these things require personal sacrifices of time, dedication, and effort. And from where does the strength and inspiration for that come?

Or, in other words, what is worth living for, sacrificing for, and even dying for?

I believe every man needs a transcendent cause. But where does that come from? Before we go on, I want to share a story with you. I hope it helps you understand what I mean by a transcendent cause.

Mogadishu, Somalia and a transcendent cause

In 1993 in Mogadishu, Somalia, I was the Delta Force commander during the events most commonly referred to as "Black Hawk Down." Two Black Hawk helicopters were shot down in the city of five million people, where most of those people were starving refugees. Within thirty minutes of the first chopper being shot down, the second one was shot down.

When the first chopper went down I sent every one of my soldiers who were already fighting in the city to rescue the crew and passengers of the first crash. I was left with few options when the second helo went down over a mile away from the first crash. I had to pull together a second rescue effort using those soldiers, sailors, and airmen who were left in the base—many of whom were not from the combat arms specialties (they were clerks, mechanics, communicators, and supply people). To their credit, every man was eager to be part of the effort to rescue their brothers at the second crash site.

Two of the Delta Force snipers, Randy Shughart and Gary Gordon, watched the second Black Hawk go down from their position in another helo. The Black Hawk helicopter carrying Shughart and Gordon was being used as an airborne sniper platform. They radioed immediately to inform us the crew in the second crash was alive but injured and it appeared they could not get themselves out of their seats. They reported, "Their backs are probably broken. Put us in and we can get them out."

The answer was immediate. "We can't send you in because we have nobody to support you with. You would be going into a hornet's nest since everybody's at the first crash site. It'll take a while to get a force together to send in there to help you out. Stay above them and keep shooting—take out as many Somalis as you can."

They did. But they called back in less than thirty minutes and said, "There are too many Somalis coming in. You've got to put us on the ground!"

The answer was "No" for the second time.

The third time they called, they sounded both adamant and desperate, "We're the only hope; put us in."

It was important to question their situational awareness regarding what was happening. Did they fully understand the risks? They reported that they were well aware of what they were going into since they were watching it unfold from their perch in the helo.

"Yes, put us in." They went in. And they fought valiantly, but both gave their lives to save one of their own.

The lone survivor from the crash told us the incredible story of Randy and Gordy, which became the narrative for the recommendations of Medals of Honor for both men. Chief Warrant Officer Michael Durant, the pilot of the crashed bird, relayed the following story.

The two snipers jumped to the ground from a lower hover of their Black Hawk and began firing on Somali militia as they fought their way into the crash site. Once at the crash site, Randy covered Gordy as Gordy helped the four crew members out of the crash. Once he had them out of the helo, he helped them find cover between the crash and a stone wall next to it.

Task accomplished, Gordy moved around the helo to help Randy engage the Somali militia determined to get to the crash. Both snipers were putting out a pretty heavy volume of fire, according to Chief Durant, until Gordy came back around to his side of the helo and asked if there was more ammo in the crashed chopper. When Durant told him to look behind the co-pilot seat, Gordy retrieved the supply and returned to Durant with a fully loaded MP5 submachine gun, laid it on Durant's chest, and said "good luck" before returning to the side where Randy was still engaging targets.

Gordy tossed ammo to Randy, who reloaded and continued firing. Moments later, Durant heard Randy yell over to his teammate, "Gordy I'm hit." His gun went silent quickly after he yelled to Gordy, and Mike Durant knew Randy Shughart was most likely dead. Only a few minutes passed before Gordy yelled in a feeble voice to Durant that he was also hit and soon it was obvious he, too, was dead. As the Somali militia swept over the crash site, they killed three of the four crew members, leaving only Chief Durant to tell the story.

I had the honor of standing in the West Wing of the White House as the U.S. president presented the medals to the widows and families of those two incredible warriors.

There is no question those two men knew they were putting their lives on the line by going into that chaotic scene. Their request was denied twice. Yet they still asked to go in. Why?

The answer is because they had a transcendent cause.

And what was that transcendent cause? In their case, it was part of the fifth stanza of the Ranger Creed: "Never shall I leave a fallen comrade to fall into the hands of the enemy." Those two men lived and died by it.

That promise to their fellow soldiers was their transcendent cause. Maybe we'd like to think it was the American flag or the U.S. Constitution or the oath they took to defend that Constitution. But, no, when you get to that level of combat, it's all about the guy on your right and the guy on your left. And your transcendent cause is the commitment you've made to each other. It's just part of who you are and what you do. You know he's not going to fail you and leave you. And he knows the same about you.

We fought an eighteen-hour battle that day. Most people don't realize this, but we were fighting over two of our dead comrades—the pilot and co-pilot. And we took more casualties because we refused to leave them behind. We couldn't get those two bodies extracted from that helicopter, and we were not going to leave the remains of our two men behind. We were fighting over dead bodies. But, to us, it didn't matter. Alive or dead, they were our comrades and they were coming out with us. We knew they would have been there for us were the roles reversed.

When Randy Shughart and Gary Gordon made that third request to go down into the street, they knew there wasn't much chance they would come out alive. That's a transcendent cause.

And so was recovering the bodies of the others who died.

The question for today is this—have we assessed our lives to determine who and what it is that's worth living and dying for? One can be part of today's "give me" generation or one can be part of "I'll give to you." Shughart and Gordon were givers—not takers. And they gave their lives. But they gave their lives because they had a transcendent cause. Their cause was—at the tactical level—the same for every warrior who's ever been on the battlefield: the guy behind you, in front of you, and on your right and left.

Risking everything to save a wingman

There's another related story, recorded in a book called *Devotion*, written by Adam Makos. It's the story of a wealthy, elite Ivy League graduate, Lieutenant Tom Hudner Jr. In 1948, Hudner was commissioned in the U.S. Navy and became a naval aviator.

Another naval aviator—a sharecropper's son out of Hattiesburg, Mississippi, Ensign Jesse Brown, was determined to become the first black naval pilot to land on the deck of a ship—and he was.

Then, in 1950, at the Chosin Reservoir, when the U.S. Marines were surrounded by three hundred thousand Chinese, the young, black aviator was shot down. And it turns out Jesse's best friend was this Ivy League, polo-playing white boy, Tom, who was flying a second airplane as Jesse's wingman.

Jesse crashed after taking several hits from anti-aircraft weapons. He went down on the side of a mountain on frozen, snow-covered terrain. The book gives a vivid description of this scenario. Jesse Brown popped the canopy off the cockpit once he crashed, but try as he might, he could not get out of the plane. He was jammed in the airplane because of metal entrapping his legs. His situation was hopeless without outside assistance, someone who could chop or cut the metal around him.

Lieutenant Tom Hudner Jr. saw what had happened. He had to make a decision and make it fast. He watched the whole thing and knew his buddy was down there trying to get out of his ruined plane. It was obvious Jesse couldn't pull himself out. Tom's decision had to be quick—he was going to run out of fuel soon. He either had to go back and refuel or try something more drastic. Tom knew to attempt to crash-land his own plane in order to help his best friend would be very risky, from many angles.

First, his chance of being killed was pretty significant, either in the crash if the plane caught fire or from being stranded on the mountain in an almost artic environment where temperatures dropped as low as thirty degrees below zero. The second reason was less important to Tom but deliberately crashing his plane, even to save his wingman, was grounds for a court martial, which could result in time in prison.

Tom quickly made the decision he had to make as a friend, and wingman. Hudner crash-landed his plane on the side of that mountain. He rushed over and tried to get Jesse out. But it was winter, and so cold he couldn't break through the metal. He was unable to release his badly injured friend from the cockpit, and, before long, Jesse Brown died.

Ultimately a U.S. Navy helicopter rescued Tom. Would he now have to defend himself before the courts? Would he do time? He failed to save Jesse Brown. What would happen now? Did Tom regret his decision; was it the right decision?

The U.S. Navy quickly provided the answer as to their view of what Tom did—he was awarded the Medal of Honor.

Why? Everybody who hears that story wonders what they would have done. Why did he do it? He did it because he had a transcendent cause. And that transcendent cause—saving his friend's life—was what he risked his own life, and future, for. To Lieutenant Hudner, trying to save Jesse Brown was worth dying for.

That aviator's courageous determination to save a human life, along with his love for his friend and brother-in-arms, were elements of his decision. Both were transcendent causes, in that they went far beyond his natural human instinct for self-protection and taking the easy way out.

In Mogadishu, the same level of life-or-death determination held true. Those two brave snipers went into the street, hoping to rescue their buddies because of their commitment to a cause that transcended their natural sense of self-protection and desire for survival. They were willing to lay down their lives for their friends. And, according to Jesus, that is the greatest love of all.

The pages of this book are intended to help you as a male—no matter what your age or position in life—to enter your God-given calling to be a Man—and, yes, with a capital "M." As a Christian believer, I am convinced the most important step you can take into real manhood is finding the transcendent cause the Creator has placed within you, and to claim it as your own.

It's going to be about far more than your own gratification, success or accomplishment. I am not suggesting God has called you to find a cause to die for or even risk your life for, although He may have done just that. But there is a calling in your life that will most likely force you to make tough decisions that can bring criticism and ridicule from the secular world. Standing for truth in a world where everything is about feelings can be costly, but that may be what you have been called to do. It may be your transcendent cause: to be a voice of truth.

Your transcendent cause is going to be much bigger than you.

It's not just about you

Even in everyday life, something bigger, deeper, and more important than self-satisfaction needs to be inside us. Having a transcendent cause is not just some vague idea in the back of our minds, something we'll hang onto just in case of a crisis or a battle. No, it has to be there day in and day out. Our lives should reflect our commitment to that cause. One example of this may be as simple is your faithfulness to some uninteresting and seemingly unrewarding job—simply because you've got to bring home a check—and not giving up on it.

Man, as a provider, should ponder what really matters in his life. Yes, think about it and give it careful consideration. Your ultimate transcendent cause should be doing the will of God. Another transcendent cause ought to be, at the very least, financial independence—for example, moving out of your parents' house. And, if you're married, it's all about supporting the woman you've married and the children you've fathered, and the obligations you've made to pay their bills. That very basic transcendent cause ought to compel you to stay in that job until you've lined up another one. And to do your best until you move on.

Now, some guys may say, "I'm quitting. It just doesn't pay enough." My response to that is, "So not working pays better?"

Maybe you *can* do better, but you need to line up another job first. Why? Because being a provider isn't just about you. You're either in this world to take or you're here to give. And if you're here to give, you're not going to leave one job until you have another one lined up (unless they fire you—sometimes that happens).

And why aren't you going to walk away from that job? Because you have obligations and those obligations can and will become a transcendent cause if you'll let them. Hopefully, it's a family, a wife, and children. But every man—and particularly every God-fearing Christian man—has the transcendent cause of keeping his commitments and meeting his financial obligations.

In fact, the Bible takes it a step further. It says, "*Whatever you do*, do it all for the glory of God" (1 Cor. 10:31 [NIV], emphasis mine).

So, let's agree that according to the Bible, men are called not only to provide for their family needs, but also the needs of those around them.

It's a biblical reality that we men will have to work and, by the sweat of our brows, we'll earn a living. That's what God told Adam, and that goes way back to the beginning of humankind. Now, of course, that's if you're able-bodied, if you're capable.

I need to qualify this because there are men who are disabled or in ill health, and I'm especially conscious of those men who were born with disabilities or are veterans of the U.S. military, or with disabilities that came about some other way.

That said, even disabled men frequently find a means of providing for their family, one way or another.

And I hope, while our minds are on financial matters, you'll be thinking ahead, giving serious thought to the future. Maybe you aren't called to be much of a provider just yet. But what about tomorrow? How in the future will you provide for yourself, the family you'll eventually have, your aging parents, and others in your circle of concern?

Deadbeat Dads and working women

There's an epidemic in the U.S. of "fatherless" children. Of course, every child had a father to begin with, but some fathers don't live long enough to see their boys grow into men. Others, thanks to divorce, are "Disneyland Dads," who occasionally take their children out for a day or two, but don't live with the family. Still others simply don't take responsibility for their sons and daughters, financially or otherwise. The absentee father fails to be a man on a mission—someone whose kids grow up with a caring, generous, and godly man, a provider in their lives. That is, most certainly, a transcendent cause—or at least it should be.

Unfortunately, all too often in cases of unwed mothers or divorced parents, fathers have a way of disappearing and leaving a huge empty place in their sons' and daughters' lives.

What does that have to do with you?

I'll give you a couple of examples of how a man can provide something invaluable to fatherless children without spending a dime.

One single mom I know told me about a man—a Christian—who owned a gym. Mark was a physical therapist and was a body-builder as a younger man. But Mark knew about more than weight training and nutrition, and he could see the woman's boys were entering their teenage years and needed some specific guidance. So, he started showing them how to put to good use the hormones surging through their adolescent bodies—how to build strength and size. He helped them with their occasional sports injuries, too, and gave them some man-to-man advice about how to deal with life in the locker room.

Mark didn't give the boys or their mom a dime and wasn't around forever. But he became an informal coach to those two teenagers for a couple of years. His cause was to make strong—and strong-looking—young men out of a couple of awkward, skinny kids. He provided just what they needed, just when they needed it.

In another case, Ryan, a fourteen-year-old, was admitted to an elite private school. His mom had very little money but knew her son was smart, hardworking, and motivated. Meanwhile, she was willing to make the extra effort to drive him to school (there was no school bus), purchase fairly expensive uniforms for him, and to otherwise encourage Ryan to fit in with his wealthy classmates as well as he could.

The extra help Ryan's mom received wasn't more financial aid. Instead, it came from the high school principal—an education-oriented man with sons of his own—who recognized the potential in the new boy on campus. He quietly began to advise him, offer encouragement, and help him find his way into a social world almost entirely made up of rich kids. By the time Ryan's senior year rolled around, thanks in large part to the quiet guidance the principal provided, he was a letterman in three sports, a straight-A student, and a respected student leader.

Neither Mark, the gym owner, nor the high school principal had a lot to gain by helping those young men. But they saw what was missing in their lives. And they provided some things money cannot buy—guidance, practical advice, life lessons, and, most of all, generous, manly encouragement.

Of course, many working women aren't single mothers. In fact, if you're the average husband, you're probably married to a woman who also brings home a paycheck.

A few Christian men I've met seem to think they are somehow robbed of their manhood if their wife has a job, and it's even worse if she has a serious career of her own. That's a foolish attitude. At the same time, what is even worse is a man whose wife is compelled to work because her husband has refused to get a job.

In today's economy, women often find it necessary to enter the workforce in order to supplement the family income. That means the man of the house needs to pitch in and provide help, sharing household chores and caring for the kids. (By the way, I really enjoyed helping with the kids, but those household chores were a problem. I cannot say I was a superstar at that.) It isn't always easy, particularly when both Mom and Dad are exhausted and there's nothing they'd rather do than watch a ball game on TV or take a nap.

Just to be clear—you aren't less of a man if your wife works. And you're doing everyone a great service—including yourself—by sharing the burdens of family responsibility. The fact is, getting through busy years with young children is everybody's job and it requires sacrifice on the part of all concerned.

When your family starts to grow and a new baby is born, while that infant is nursing, the mother needs to be with her child. I think that's the way it should be, but once the baby has been weaned, if your wife wants or needs to return to work, that's a choice you and she need to make. Just be sure you're both able to spend as much time as possible with the kids during their formative years.

It bears repeating—I would hate to see a woman who's forced to work because her husband refuses to provide for his family.

A working woman's success story

That raises another question—what happens when a wife becomes more successful than her husband? I've never been in that position, but I would assume it could be a difficult issue for some men. On the other hand, some husbands are quite pleased because their wife's success encourages them to work hard, too, both at their place of employment and in the household.

My brother, Blake, is a good example. He retired from his job because his wife became the CEO of a big corporation. When she landed the job he said, "In that case, I am retiring, and I'll take care of things at home."

He is quite happy with that. He doesn't feel diminished at all. He believes in working together as a team and he's playing an important part in providing for her in any way he can. He was a successful businessman; he owned his own business—a sporting goods store. But when she took the new job, he was man enough to say, "I'm going to help you be successful."

So, my brother is providing for his successful wife in a different way than financially. He's providing encouragement and support for her while she uses her gifts. He's always at her side at social activities. And he's very quick to say, "I retired so I can support her!"

A man's healthy sense of self—along with a dose of humility—means he can provide far more than money to those he cares for, whether for a season or for a lifetime.

Social welfare vs. personal provision

From a financial perspective, if you're a provider and you're able to provide, it's up to you to give something back from what you earn. You can do this through your church, by offering a tithe—10 percent of your earnings as an offering of gratitude to the Lord. It is a biblical mandate to tithe. Beyond your tithe, you should give as you can to worthy causes but that does not mean you have to give away more than you're able. Quite the contrary—first and foremost, you have a responsibility to take care of your family.

You can do a self-evaluation—how much are you spending on your golf game? Or your hunting and fishing hobby? Could some portion of that be used to support the local Boys and Girls Club in your community? Maybe just ten or twenty dollars a month? If you're able to give to the less fortunate, you're fulfilling a biblical principal of "providing" for the needy. Nowadays, monthly donations to help the poor are less common than they used to be.

One of the biggest reasons for the gradual erosion of charitable giving is the social welfare system. Social welfare is nothing new in America. Four hundred years ago, the first English colony at Jamestown, Virginia, tried a socialist system. The Virginia company back in London owned the land and all its produce and everybody got an equal share out of the common store of food. Yet this system destroyed the incentive to work. In fact, many Jamestown settlers looked for gold or bowled in the streets rather than worked in the fields because they knew they had their share of food coming regardless. Predictably, the food ran out and many starved and died. In less than a year, the colony dwindled from 104 down to 38 souls. After another boatload from England arrived to bolster their numbers, Captain John Smith, a real man's man, took over leadership of the failing colony in September 1608, and declared:

> [T]hink not that either my pains, nor the [investors'] purses, will ever maintain you in idleness and sloth… [T]he greater part must be more industrious, or starve…[Y]ou must obey this now for a Law, that he that will not work shall not eat (except by sickness he be disabled) for the labors of thirty or forty honest

and industrious men shall not be consumed to maintain an [sic] hundred and fifty idle loiterers…"[1]

Notice, Captain Smith decreed, "He that will not work, shall not eat." Sound familiar? It's from the Bible (2 Thess. 3:10). Not too surprisingly, under Smith's firm leadership, the death toll dropped, relations with the natives stayed mostly at an uneasy truce, the fort was repaired and expanded, crops were planted, a well dug, trees cut into clapboards, and products such as pitch, tar, and soap ash were produced for shipment back to England. Eventually, the socialist plan was ditched as plots of land were granted, contributions to the common store decreased, and every man enjoyed the fruit of his labor. As a result, production exploded, and the Virginia colony became wildly successful. Ah, the miracle of capitalism fueled by the biblical principle of work and its just reward!

Today some think we are smarter than our ancestors with all the cries for socialism. The return toward a socialist welfare system during the Great Depression was led by President Franklin Delano Roosevelt. With each successive generation and political administration, we tax those who will work and redistribute it to those who won't work. We are drifting closer and closer to the failure of early Jamestown. If you go into the neighborhoods across America, especially the ones we call "the hood," you'll probably notice groups of unemployed men standing on the street corners, smoking cigarettes, or groups of gangbangers roaming the streets, dealing drugs and making trouble.

All too often, that's because it's more advantageous for them not to work. And instead, many of them are turning to drugs and alcohol.

As a man, have you ever struggled to make ends meet, or even been down and out for a while? If so, you know how important it is to have someone come along and provide a shoulder to lean on. As the old saying goes, "Men don't want a handout, they just need a hand up."

This isn't necessarily about you giving money away. It's also about providing friendship, kindness, and encouragement. That's so important. It is also a matter of offering dignity, self-respect, and honor. Lots of struggling men don't realize what's happened to them, and the reality is, social welfare is hurting them because it's robbing them of their God-given reason for living as well as their dignity.

Until FDR implemented his welfare state, churches and caring Christians took on the responsibility of taking care of people. Even now, you'll still find many churches with community outreaches— they run a soup kitchen, or they provide programs to help needy people, especially during times of disaster. But, unfortunately, some churches have abrogated their responsibility and handed it over to the government.

Don't get me wrong—there's definitely a place for welfare— as a temporary provision. Before we were married, my wife was a single mother with two children. There were difficult times when she needed the help of the social welfare system so she could get on her feet, break away from that vicious cycle, and reclaim her independence. She fought hard to do that, and once she did, she never looked back.

However, for any number of reasons, some people are unable to make it without help of one kind or another. And as a man—a provider—you have an obligation to help care for those who can't take care of themselves. Maybe there's a homeless shelter near you, or a veterans' rehab center. Or perhaps your church may sponsor a Christian program that assists truly disabled, handicapped, or elderly men, women, or children. By finding time to care for them, you'll be offering a gift of dignity and respect. And, in doing so, you will be living up to the godly values He has placed within you.

Men with good values

It is a man's responsibility to provide values to his family and others. The very best way for you to provide values is by embodying them and living your values in the presence of those around you.

But what are "values" in the first place?

I may know your name, and I may even know a little bit about your life. But what are your values? Your values undergird what people see you do and what they judge you by. Essentially, the values you live by are a kind of identity—your values represent who you are. It's a strange thing, though, that many people can't articulate their values. They've never had to. They may say, "I'm going to vote for the person who best represents my values." Well, what are those values? What is one issue you care about?

"Well, my candidate wants to improve the highways in the state."

Oh really? So that's what you call your values? Still, truthfully, it isn't always easy to think about the values we consider most important in our lives.

How about if I give you some ideas to start with? In no particular order, here are some words usually considered essential Christian values. You may consciously recognize some of them as being part of who you are. And, like most of us, you may notice you're lacking in a few others.

- Gratitude
- Courage (physical and moral)
- Patriotism
- Persistence
- Grace
- Love
- Humility
- Patience
- Kindness
- Mercy
- Diligence
- Faith and Faithfulness
- Generosity
- Trust and Trustworthiness
- Morality
- Purity
- Vision

Those words represent some of the core values that shape us into the people we are. Each of us is likely to embody some of those qualities more than others. But, as men, we are also meant to provide those values to those around us—starting with family, then extending into our other circles of influence.

A great example of that is my close friend, Stu Weber. His Christian values come through in his actions and words. You would expect that from a pastor, but so many pastors today have compromised on key biblical issues. Stu also reflects an incredible love for America. His patriotism is so obvious. He values America and knows our history and the sacrifices made to allow us to be the nation we are. I love and appreciate him for that because there is a serious effort in the nation today to destroy our pride in being Americans.

When people kneel for the national anthem, desecrate the flag, and refuse to recite the Pledge of Allegiance, we have a problem. Stu wears his value of love for the nation on his sleeve, so to speak. And another friend, Yale King, is a man who never served in the military, but you only need to be around him for five minutes and you will see his deep love for the nation regardless of how well he knows you. He is a self-made man who left home at fourteen years old, eventually co-founded a major rental car company, and has lived the American dream. His values start with love for his nation and a strong work ethic.

How about you? Do people see your values reflected in your life? Do you provide an example of positive values for those around you? You should. Don't fall prey to the notion that you should not push your values on others. I disagree. If your vales are those of faith and patriotism, you need to stand for them publicly, and speak truth to a society where fact now matters less than feelings.

You may have noticed one of the values I listed is vision. The Bible says, "My people perish for lack of vision" (Prov. 29:18 [KJV]). We must have vision ourselves. There's no successful organization in America—whether it's a church, a business, or a family that's reaching its full potential—not founded and influenced by someone of vision.

Vision means looking past the daily grind, or your ordinary routine and habit patterns—even pulling yourself out of feelings of doubt or fear—and "seeing" yourself and your place in the world from a different angle. Vision is a fresh perspective; it means expanding your horizons. Vision is looking at "the big picture" and attempting to see into the future, regarding goals and objectives to be achieved.

Men of vision

I think some people are more visionary than others. Exceptional vision is a God-given gift. As men, we have some responsibility for providing vision. Whether you're a CEO or a student leader or a pastor or in military service or a husband and father, at some point it's going to be up to you to provide vision—that big picture—for those around you. Let me give you an example.

Think about the dad who has to go home and say, "Kids, we're moving."

"No! We can't move! Are you serious?"

"Yes, I'm very serious! I've been given an offer I believe is consistent with what the Lord wants for us as a family, and we're moving."

"I don't want to leave my friends!"

"Well, I appreciate that, and I wouldn't want to either. But… we're moving."

Does that conversation require courage? Yeah, I think it does, because it would be far easier to just say, "Nah, I don't want to upset them, and they're not going to be happy."

Well, if you have vision for yourself or your family, and, if you really believe there's an opportunity you'll regret not pursuing, you're looking at the big picture. You're operating as a visionary for your wife and kids.

In that case, you'll tell your son or daughter, "I'm going to be able to afford to send you to a good college in a few years."

Or, "I'm going to be able to send you to a good summer camp where you'll get a chance to learn basketball, and maybe even a little Scripture."

Essentially, here's what you're saying: "The reason we're having this conversation is I have a new vision for our family, and it's going to give us opportunities we didn't have before."

Does giving direction or providing vision require courage or strength? I don't think there's any question about that. Courage and strength can be gained by *just doing it*. It's always easier the second time. The hardest decision is the first one. What is your vision, and who are you supposed to provide that vision to?

With that said, how do you gain that kind of strength? First of all, don't make a decision you haven't thought through and you haven't prayed about. If it's the kind of decision that's impacting the family or affecting the community and others around you, make sure you've carefully thought it through.

As a parent or a concerned adult, are you able to provide vision to young students? Can you help them see why learning matters and how it's going to benefit them in the future? "Dad, why should we study history? I don't like history." Or, "Dad, why do I need a science class? I'm not going to be a scientist."

You are at least one of the people who casts a vision for how today's educational tasks will help that young person in the future. That responsibility is not unique to men, but it certainly is something men should be able to provide.

So, what about you? How do you develop the kind of vision you need to provide for those around you? I believe you develop that vision through prayer. And you develop that vision through talking to people older and wiser than yourself, and by reading, studying, and knowing history. History often provides a foundation for future vision. Sadly, we are grossly ignorant of our history as a nation because of the modern public education system, which has either altered or totally ignored history.

And what about the church? Who are the people with a vision for the church? Well, you start with the pastor, but you've got to also have elders in the church who can either catch that vision and share it or provide an alternative vision. The pastor may be 80 percent of the solution in terms of a vision for the church. The people he brings around him, specifically the elders and the rest of his staff, are there to help him with that last 20 percent.

Because of my military background and service as a commander, there have been times I've had to focus on the big picture and make, and communicate, very difficult decisions—I've described one of them at the beginning of this chapter. Every man who's had to command troops in combat has had to look at the big picture.

When Harry Truman made the decision to drop atomic bombs on Japan, he didn't do that assuming he wasn't going to be criticized for it. He was looking at ending the war and saving a million American lives. He provided vision for the nation in spite of the fact that many criticized him then and even more do now.

And what about Winston Churchill? He let the Germans bomb the British city of Coventry to protect the fact that the Allies had broken the German's code. He allowed the Germans to bomb Coventry because he was looking strategically at ending the war. And he knew if he let it be known that he was reading the Germans' mail, they would immediately change their code.

That's thinking strategically versus looking at the tactical situation. I think everybody who's ever commanded troops has had to look at circumstances strategically. And that amounts to having vision.

A man provides identity

Although my dad, Cecil, never finished high school, he was a man of wisdom. As we drove the eighty miles from our home in New Bern, North Carolina, to my grandparents' home in Wilson, North Carolina, my dad told me about my family tree. He would say things like "Jerry, your great grandfather on Papa Boykin's side was named Richmond Irving Boykin, and he raised tobacco in Nash county. He loved music and played a fiddle left-handed. He married Suzy Williamson, who was only four-feet, eleven-inches tall and was known as 'the best biscuit maker in Wilson county.'" Then Dad went through the brothers and sisters of both of his grandparents before he switched over to my mom's side and went through the same detailed discussion of who they were. I found it boring and failed to see the utility of it until years later. What was I to do with all this talk about people I didn't know?

Dad was giving me an identity, something that would make clear what the Boykin name meant in the area he grew up in. He would go into detail about the two Boykin brothers who were given a land grant in Isle of Wight county, Virginia, in the early 1600s. The small community of Boykin, Virginia, was where they settled and began the history of the Boykin family in America.

How many children today have no identity because they don't even know who their fathers are? Dad was proud of his family even though they were simple farmers. They were salt-of-the-earth, hard-working people with strong values of faith, family, and country, and

Cecil wanted me to know and appreciate where I came from, what my family history was, and what he thought was important about my lineage.

I am one of those who usually skipped over the chapters in the Bible listing the descendants or the sons of a certain biblical character. It was boring, and I knew I would not remember any of it. But then it dawned on me: God was showing the importance of knowing your bloodline. It was critical for the Jews in biblical times just as it is now. To be considered a member of a tribe, a Jew had to know and be able to prove his lineage back at least two generations. Today, Jews making *Aliyah,* or returning to Israel to establish citizenship, must be able to prove they are Jews.

Knowing where you come from is important, and I learned that again as I watched my wife search for two years for her family. Ashley and her twin sister were adopted at nine weeks old in Manhattan. She always wondered about her bloodline but had no way of finding out since the records in New York were sealed. Then Ancestry.com offered her new hope for finding her identity. After a DNA test, she was connected to her relatives. The passion with which she pursued her identity was incredible. It was watching her as she went through this process that made me realize how important identity really is when you don't have one, or you don't know your family history.

Ashley was so overjoyed when it all came together for her. But there are many Ashleys out there who need to know their identities. Fathers and grandfathers need to very consciously and deliberately study, and know, their family history and lineage. Then they should share that with the generations behind them—the children and grandchildren. Make it a point to discuss their identity with them and share some history.

What if there are things to be ashamed of in the family history? You know, like Grandpa was a bootlegger? Well, at least mine was—on my mother's side. He was one of the largest peddlers of illegal whiskey in his state, North Carolina, during prohibition. But it is still part of my family history, and knowing it gives me the opportunity to establish a new legacy.

If you don't know your identity, can't identify your roots, or can't relate to your history, then start to investigate it. A man must provide identity to the family. If you are adopted, as my wife is, you may or may not find your lineage. If you don't, then start thinking about what you want your grandchildren to remember about your family values and history. Create a legacy that reflects the Judeo-Christian roots of America and the Christian values of the family.

Our model and His transcendent cause

We all need to recognize our own transcendent cause. Whatever your status in life, whether you're single or married, you are called to be a provider. Because that's what a man does—a man is a provider. And, as we'll see in the following pages, he is meant to be that and much more.

But, married or single, retired or working, healthy or disabled, there is an even greater transcendent cause.

There was one Man who came down and died for all of us one time, wasn't there? Every time I read that old story, the part that fascinates me most is when Jesus knelt there in the Garden of Gethsemane and said, "O my Father, if this cup may not pass away from me, except I drink it, thy will be done" (Matt. 26:42 [KJV]).

He already knew what a miserable death he was about to endure. Yet, he still said, "Not as I will, but as thou wilt" (Matt. 26:39 [KJV]). He was saying the same thing the prophet Isaiah said centuries before, "Here am I; send me" (Isaiah 6:8 [KJV]).

As men—as Christian men—we are modeling ourselves after Christ's example. We have to be willing to go the distance, to know what it is we're willing to sacrifice for and die for. Some men have no idea what that means because they've never thought about it. They haven't yet been put to the test.

Many men have never been taken to the edge.

If you don't know what you believe, or, more importantly, why you believe it, or value it, or why it's precious to you, it's unlikely you're going to have a transcendent cause.

On the other hand, maybe you've thought all that through and have come up with answers to some hard questions. *Why* do I believe that? *How* do I know that's true? *What* do I value above all else? And—most important of all—*Who* is the source of my strength and courage? Once you've found satisfying answers to those questions, your transcendent cause will become increasingly clear.

That cause—*His* cause—and the vision it provides, will equip you with the strength and courage you need. With His help, you'll become the man and provider your Creator designed you to be.

MAN AS THE PROVIDER—
A WORD FOR WOMEN

Since you're reading this book, there's most likely at least one very important male in your life. If you're a mom, you'll find some useful information to share with your growing boys as they move into becoming godly men. And, if you're married or preparing for your wedding, I hope you'll give some thought to the ideas General Boykin has provided in these pages and how you might be able to put them to good use.

In today's world, many men are feeling exceptionally conflicted because of controversies about masculinity, and how "maleness" should, and shouldn't, be expressed. For Christians, there are also questions about how the biblical role of a man should look.

As for being a "provider," we all know successful male-female relationships don't work very well if they're one-sided. In our very demanding world, roles in the family often shift. For instance, if a husband has gone back to school to earn a graduate degree, his wife may well be bringing home a significant part of the family income. If she, on the other hand, falls ill or has just given birth to a child—or if she's working on a project that requires her full attention—a husband's role may be unusually focused around providing help with tasks his wife normally accomplishes.

In everyday life for healthy couples, many responsibilities are shared. I hope that's what you're experiencing. When you think about it, what are you currently providing—or helping provide—for your household? What do you currently do to support your partner so he can provide for your family in the way you and he think best? And what could you do to provide more support for him?

Communication is incredibly important as couples and families work out the details of daily living. Are you able to communicate openly with the man in your life about tasks, responsibilities, or projects in which you might feel a need for more support from him? And is he able to tell you comfortably and without feeling uneasy what he wishes you might do to offer a little more help to him in some area?

Additionally, if the man in your life has gone above and beyond the call of duty to provide for you in a special way, I hope you've wholeheartedly expressed your gratitude. In fact, you and he might want to thank God together for each other and for the blessings you're enjoying because of the reciprocal efforts you're making in your homelife.

MAN AS THE PROVIDER—
DISCUSSION QUESTIONS

1. What did you learn from the General's father Cecil about what it means to be a provider for your family?

2. Being a provider requires personal sacrifice of time, dedication, and effort. Have you assessed your life to determine who and what is worth living for, sacrificing for, and even dying for? Do you have a transcendent cause? If so, what is it? How does it involve those close to you? How can you make sure your life reflects your commitment to your transcendent cause?

3. Man, as a provider, should take care of his family and seek to meet their needs. Ponder the general's statement, "Being a provider isn't just about you. You are either in this world to take or you're here to give." How does that impact how you look at your current job(s)?

4. Have you ever considered your work as part of your worship? Meditate on 1 Corinthians 10:31 (NIV), "Whatever you do, do it all for the glory of God." How should that verse impact your performance on the job?

5. Recalling the story of Mark, the gym owner, how could you invest in the life of a child with an absent dad? Do you know someone in your extended family, your church, or community to whom you can be a blessing in that way?

6. As a man—a provider—you have an obligation to help care for those who can't take care of themselves. What are some specific things you can do in your community to help people in need?

7. As a man, it is your responsibility to provide values to your family and others. What values are most important to you? What values need to be shored up in your own life from the list? What values do you want to pass on to your children and families? And lastly, how do these values line up with the issues we are facing in society today?

8. Now that you've discussed which values you would like to pass on to your children and families, ask yourself, "Do people see my values reflected in the way I live my life? Do I provide an example of positive values for those around me?"

9. This chapter also talks about providing vision, a big picture for those you lead. What is your vision of a preferred future for yourself, your marriage, your family, or your team? It is important to develop and refine your vision through prayer. Take some time to pray it over, think it through, and write it down. Clarify it before you communicate it.

10. As a provider, it is important to provide identity for your family. Reflect on how General Boykin's dad, Cecil, did it. What are some specific and creative ways you could do this for your family? Might it involve a road trip? A heritage hunt over a weekend or maybe a family vacation where you track down parts of your family identity?

CHAPTER TWO

MAN AS AN INSTRUCTOR

I would advise no one to send his child where the Holy Scriptures are not supreme. Every institution that does not unceasingly pursue the study of God's word becomes corrupt.... I greatly fear that the universities, unless they teach the Holy Scriptures diligently and impress them on the young students, are wide gates to hell.

—Martin Luther²

Preach the word; be prepared in season and out of season; correct, rebuke and encourage—with great patience and

*careful instruction. For the time will come when people
will not put up with sound doctrine. Instead, to suit their
own desires, they will gather around them a great number
of teachers to say what their itching ears want to hear.*

—*2 Timothy 4:2 (NIV)*

When I was a young lieutenant, the U.S. Army founded what has become one of the most famous and renowned organizations in the military today: the U.S. Army Ranger Battalions. Up until then, there were some small Ranger units in Vietnam, but this was going to be a contemporary, modern, post-Vietnam Ranger battalion.

U.S. Army Chief of Staff General Creighton W. Abrams ordered the activation of the first Ranger battalion in 1973 at Fort Stewart, Georgia. I was blessed to be a part of it. We would fall out in formation on the parade grounds at Fort Stewart, and the commander of that unit, Lieutenant Colonel Kenneth Leuer, would stand on an elevated platform before we did our morning exercise, and he would recite the history from which we derived our lineage. And he would say, "Gentlemen, we are descendants of Merrill's Marauders. The Marauders' motto was *sua sponte*, 'of my own accord.' It could be translated as, 'This I freely give.'"

Merrill's Marauders were in the jungles of Burma for ten months, fighting behind Japanese lines to open a road through the jungle to China. They were there to deliver aid to General Chiang Kai-shek's

Nationalist Army, which was locked in a stalemate with the Imperial Japanese Army. They went into that jungle with three thousand men and they came out less than a year later with three hundred. On their own accord, they sacrificed themselves.

I was not the only young officer who began to take pride in our forebears and their exploits. Everybody out there on that field realized the fact that we were the descendants—we were the next generation—of these great men who did incredible things. We all wanted to be just like them, to do anything we could to preserve their memory and live up to their legacy because we were the descendants of Merrill's Marauders.

Leuer would go on to say the first three battalion commanders were Osborne, McGee, and Beech. "OMB," he would say. "Office, Management, and Budget—same three letters." That was the way he'd get us to remember those commanders' names. Then we would recite the Ranger Creed every morning.

The Battalion commander was making the point that history was just as important as physical training. Only after he gave us the history did our physical training begin. And sometimes it was brutal.

LTC Leuer realized how important it was for us to understand the proud tradition of this unit being formed. He believed it was important for us to know the history of our forebears, of those who went before us. Look today at the incredible combat record of the Rangers and how they have fought against incredible odds—they've fought sacrificially, and they've also had a very high casualty rate. But their history has been carried on and passed down from generation to generation to those who followed us after we created the first Ranger Battalion.

Why did that history help us as young warriors fulfill our military assignments with dedication, determination, and courage? Because our commander was making us more than aware that we were walking in the footsteps of fabled American heroes and we were meant to live up to their example. He wanted us to realize their history would soon be our history.

Encouraging men to be real men

In the military, the drill instructor may not be the most popular guy in the world. And when I say a man should be an *Instructor*, that's not the kind of instructor I'm talking about. Maybe you'd rather think of yourself as a professor, a teacher, a tutor, or whatever you want to call it. But a non-military instructor's responsibility is to educate and encourage his family, friends, and peers and to provide valuable ideas, facts, and insights whenever he has the opportunity. To share his wisdom and lessons learned is critical to the development of the next generation.

We want our children and our grandchildren to know about the realities of life in this world. We hope to equip them with facts that will help them realize who they are, what their responsibilities are, and who and what came before them. We want them to be proud of their God-given identities and carry on the legacy and the traditions of their forebears. We hope someday they'll share those things with their own children.

We also want to inspire other men—friends and colleagues, fellow churchgoers, students, veterans, retirees, whomever we can reach within our circles of influence—to take their place as God's men. Nothing could be more important in this troubled world than for serious, godly men to step up in such a time as this.

Now this doesn't mean a man needs to turn into a know-it-all, behaving like one of those guys who can't help but interrupt everybody to make sure we all know he's an expert. You've run into that guy, haven't you? No, what I mean by being an instructor is just as much about listening, studying, and determining what needs to be said as it is about offering facts and information. I cannot overemphasize the importance of studying, especially history, in order to be the man who can provide relevant and timely information and advice to any discussion. More on that later.

My mentor for almost forty years was one of those great warriors Ken Leuer told us about, a member of Merrill's Marauder's, retired Lieutenant General Samuel V. Wilson—General Sam, as he was known. He was almost a second father to me. The man lived so many lives in his ninety-five years I hardly knew where to start when I did his eulogy in June 2017. He was a Special Forces commander, a spy for both the CIA and the Defense Intelligence Agency, and an attaché in Moscow for many years. He was gentle and perceptive yet lethal when necessary.

I spent many hours throughout those years just talking to him about myriad topics, but mostly about warfare, human nature, and faith. He would sit patiently and listen while nodding periodically to let me know he was following my reasoning, even when I knew it was not particularly coherent. When I finished, and only then, he responded. His southside Virginia drawl made you think you were listening to Thomas Jefferson.

His thoughts were focused and reflected that he had heard everything I said. He was a master storyteller, who could keep his listener hanging on every word, and he often used stories to respond to my thoughts and questions. Every story had a lesson and a message with deep meaning. I so miss him and his counsel, but he left me with a desire to be like him and to pass on wisdom to the next generation. Men need to do that. Men need a General Sam in their lives.

To get started, we're going to look at today's "identity culture" and some of the destructive attacks men and masculinity are facing right now. There are many important reasons for men to strengthen, inspire, and equip other men for their godly responsibilities in the world. In today's society, instruction, advice, and motivation—offered man to man—become more important with every passing day.

How do I identify myself?

These days a lot of people are focused on group identity and what it means to them. We hear a lot of talk about identifying with some cause, some role, some behavior, some ethnicity, some form of victimhood, and becoming part of a like-minded group. Maybe it's sort of like creating a pseudo-family. But sadly, our current culture is so focused on specific identities it's becoming extremely polarized, as people defensively and aggressively identify with their so-called "intersectional" groups. Can we find a way to turn identity into something good?

There was a time when I would say, "If you're going to identify me with any group, make it Christians." These days, I'm not even sure I want to use that as an identity role for myself. The fact is, "Christianity" doesn't necessarily mean what it did when I was growing up.

Christianity is a choice, but at this point you have whole denominations who are approving and promoting too many unholy and unbiblical things. So, when you say, "Are you one of *those* Christians?" I don't really know what you mean. Why? Because I don't know what you think a Christian is. To make matters worse, I don't know which one of those groups you're actually talking about. In fact, I'm at the point where I'm not sure I even want you to use that term to identify me.

But if you ask me if I'm a follower of Jesus? Yes, I most certainly am. And do I know Him, love Him, and trust Him? Absolutely.

I'm also always glad to identify as a soldier. A soldier belongs to a profession and a category of people who are still reasonably respected. I think it does identify you for having made a commitment to our country, to the people of our country, and to the Constitution. It's a choice, and it's a good one.

Being a soldier was my highest goal in life when I left the gridiron of Virginia Tech and graduated from the university in December 1970. I was commissioned upon graduation as an officer in the U.S.

Army. Finally, I was seeing my dream come true. At last I was following in the footsteps of my dad, Cecil.

I was proud to be identified as a soldier in spite of the fact there were still anti-Vietnam protests all over the nation. I was grieved by that but still proud to be known and identified as a soldier. The history and legacy of soldiers meant something to me because my dad made sure I knew about the sacrifices of his generation. One of those moments, when I felt the greatest pride in being identified as an American soldier, was on Christmas Eve in 1989.

In late December that year, President George H.W. Bush sent the Delta Force, along with elements of two U.S. Army divisions, into Panama to protect the American military stationed there after a young American naval officer was killed by the Panamanian police.

Panama's dictator, Manuel Noriega, was an evil man who stole the government from the people and was ruling as a brutal tyrant. Our mission was to protect the Americans, capture Noriega, and bring him to justice. At the same time, we were to return Panama to the people.

The action started on the evening of December 20th with U.S. Military forces seizing the airports and seaports and hitting key Panamanian targets. We also launched operations to capture Noriega. As we hit more and more places where Noriega was known to hide out, he was forced to take refuge in the Vatican Embassy. Known as the *nunciatura*, the papal nuncio provided a safe haven for the outlaw dictator on Christmas Eve. We immediately sealed him in by constructing concertina wire fences and barricades around the *nunci-atura*, which was located in a fairly prominent part of the city.

That night I began to walk the perimeter, checking security and speaking to the troops who were standing guard. The Panamanian homes were decorated with colored lights and beautiful tropical flowers. It was Christmas Eve in Panama, and I thought about what my family back home was doing that evening as they gathered around the fireplace and sang carols. I missed them, and I yearned to be with them.

Only a few minutes after I began my tour around the perimeter, a Panamanian woman came out of one of the very nice homes and approached me. I wasn't sure what her purpose was, and I was cautious. She could tell in the dim light I was a bit anxious. Did she present a threat to me? Was she angry Americans were in Panama? Did she support Noriega?

As she got closer, I could see her eyes were filled with tears. Then, as she approached, she broke into a beautiful smile as she said in a joyful voice "Merry Christmas, my friend, and welcome to Panama." She reached out for my hand, and I realized instantly she wanted to share her feelings with me. Once more her eyes filled with tears as she said in an emotional voice, "Thank you, sir, for giving us our country back. May God bless you. Please come into my home and call your family on this Christmas Eve. I have many sweets you can eat. Meet my family."

Her last entreaty was for naught because her children began to exit the door of their home and proceed over to us. They all welcomed and thanked me as their mother did. After a few minutes, I thanked them all for their kindness and excused myself to continue inspecting the perimeter.

Less than five minutes later, the same scenario repeated itself and another Panamanian man and his daughter approached me with similar expressions of gratitude. After I finished my walk around, I went back into our command post and sat quietly alone and pondered what had just occurred. I decided right then as I sat there alone, this was a great Christmas Eve. I was proud to be an American, and I was very grateful I had the privilege of being called a soldier. It was the way I wanted others to see me.

Today's assault on masculinity

How about being identified as a man? Not so long ago, it might have seemed like the most natural thing in the world. And since it's pretty obvious by looking at most of us, identifying ourselves as men would have been rather unnecessary.

But today, thanks to progressive "social justice" movements, being proud and confident to identify as a man has become controversial. These days, encouraged by radical feminists and LGBTQ activists, being a man is often declared a flaw and an impairment. In fact, masculinity is sometimes even dismissed as a "toxic" condition.

Meanwhile, if we read the Bible and learn about the men of God whose stories are told there, we get a very different picture. We also get some important instructions about resisting the ways of the world—today and always, " Do not conform to the pattern of this world, but be transformed by the renewing of your mind. Then you will be able to test and approve what God's will is—his good, pleasing and perfect will" (Rom. 12:2 [NIV]).

I believe it's God's will for men to become the kind of men He created them to be. And that's what this book is all about.

Meanwhile, the battleground of identity politics is a treacherous place. The social justice warriors fighting against biblical principles in the culture wars identify as radical Hindus, progressive socialists, Marxists, homosexual activists, and countless other labels. And it's a dangerous conflict—even for them. For example, why is the feminist movement now fighting against the transgender movement?

It's because the feminists say, "No, you're not a woman. *I'm* a woman. Just because you 'feel' like a woman does not make you a woman. So, get over it."

The transgender person responds, "Every woman doesn't have a vagina."

Well, the feminists aren't having it. "Oh yes, they do! And they were born with it too, by the way."

There's no doubt about it, when it comes to today's culture wars, we men are in the line of fire. And why has this happened? An article by John Hawkins in PJ Media offers five reasons:

- Feminism is now centered on getting special privileges and man-hating.
- Fewer men see themselves as capable of being masculine.

- Traditional men don't fit into America's victim-oriented culture.
- Divorce and single moms are factors.
- The contributions of traditional men are habitually ignored.[3]

Along similar lines, Michael Gurian, a clinical therapist, recently wrote in *The Federalist*:

> Males, we are told, are born with dominion created by their inherent privilege; females (and males) are victims of this male privilege. The authors…discuss what they see as the main problem facing males—too much masculinity. They call it the root of all or most male issues from suicide to early death to depression to substance abuse to the reason for family breakups to school failure to violence. They claim that fewer males than females seek out therapy or stay in therapy and health services because of "masculinity."[4]

As an instructor or teacher, it's a man's job to instill biblical values and the responsibilities of masculinity in his family and church, among his friends, and to those with whom he has influence. It's our duty to tear down the web of lies our poisonous culture is weaving, which are meant to entrap and disable boys and men. It's up to us as traditional men to defy the world's unholy tactics, to be "transformed by the renewing of our minds," and to speak God's truth, informing, instructing, and defending one another, man to man.

The fact is, without understanding God's plan for males and females and His purpose for masculinity, young boys are far less likely to grow into healthy, strong, and influential men. Worse, they will not be prepared to take on their biblical responsibility as husbands, fathers, and leaders. At the same time, our culture will become increasingly feminized, to the detriment of our communities, schools, and workplaces. In fact, believe it or not, I think, ultimately, feminization can become a threat even to our national security.

William Kilpatrick described this serious risk in a *Crisis Magazine* article. Think about this:

> Islam, which is a hypermasculine religion, is the world's fastest growing religion. Indeed, its appeal to basic masculine psychology is one of the chief reasons for its success. In military-like summer camps across the Islamic world, young boys are taught who their enemies are, and they are taught survival skills, hand-to-hand combat, and weapons use. Along with developing fighting skills, the boys also develop a sense of camaraderie and even brotherhood. And, because the training includes religious study, they often acquire a sense of transcendent purpose. Because this type of life—let's call it "purpose-driven strife"—is highly appealing to many young men, the jihad doesn't have a recruitment problem.[5]

And while we're thinking about the impression religion can make on our youth, I hate to have to say it, but the feminizing of men and boys has entered the Christian world as well. In fact, sad as it is, in some church circles, the person of Jesus Christ is introduced—in story, sacred art, and song—as effeminate.

And that's just wrong.

Jesus was a strong, physically resilient man. He's described as a carpenter who worked with his hands to construct houses and furniture. He was a builder, and in the first century, he would also have needed to work with stone. Some historians have even described him as a stone mason—that's what builders did in those days.

Jesus was a robust, rugged man from Nazareth, a simple village offering few comforts to its working class. He had to have stamina to survive his desert ordeal, fasting for forty days during his temptation. He needed physical endurance to make the long walk from Nazareth to Jerusalem three times a year and in all kinds of weather to celebrate the Jewish holidays. We know He spent time with fishermen—a rugged and smelly crowd. We also have been told he was capable of dangerously wielding a whip when needed.

The effeminate, "pale Galilean" who appears in some Sunday school portraits and descriptions of Jesus, is a false image of the man God embodied to live in this world for thirty-three grueling years. The Jesus who walked this earth was a man's man. He is our model for manhood in particular and for living a life pleasing to God in general. That's why Peter, one of those tough fishermen, tells us Jesus left an example and we should "follow in his steps" (1 Pet. 2:21

[NIV]). That is simply biblical history and not speculation. The man who acts as an instructor needs to share that with his children and with others he influences. And yes, guys, that means *you*!

As men who are followers of Jesus, we're responsible for bringing up our children in the ways of the Lord, and we're meant to be instructors and encouragers to other men. For that reason, the Bible is the most important book in the world for us—not just for our own sake but for what we are able to offer others.

From Genesis to Revelation, in the pages of the Bible, we discover the real, earthy, and sometimes rough men and women God chose and called. We see how He led them in life and death, in love and war. Across many centuries, he raised up unlikely heroes, who continue to set an example for us, even now.

I can't encourage you enough to read and study the Bible. Here's one good reason: "For the word of God is alive and active. Sharper than any double-edged sword, it penetrates even to dividing soul and spirit, joints and marrow; it judges the thoughts and attitudes of the heart." That's from Hebrews 4:12 (NIV).

A lot of us grew up with the King James Version, and its language is beautiful. But I do find it easier to read some of the more modern translations. I read God's Word every day and I hope you do, too. I strongly recommend you buy a good commentary that provides insights into the history, context, and deep meaning of each passage.

We're living in a time when our biblical faith is in direct conflict with the ways of the world. That conflict has found its way into the classroom, into the courtroom, and at times into physical confrontations in the streets. We have to know, understand, and be confident in what we believe. That's the only way we can remain solid in our faith, which is under attack daily, both openly and underhandedly. As men who are meant to encourage and build up the faith of others, we need the sturdiest possible foundation, which can only be found in the Word of God.

Our country continues to fight wars to defend the United States from radical cultures threatening our fundamental freedoms. Our enemies—radical Islamists, Marxists, and totalitarians, to name the most obvious—are not only working against us across the seas; their emissaries are already in our midst. Of course, we need a strong fighting force abroad. But we also need smart, well-informed voices boldly speaking the truth in schools and universities, in our justice system, media, political parties, intelligence agencies, and corporations.

And most of all, we need those voices in our *homes*. And men, that means *you*—you're the instructor.

If you're going to be an effective instructor to those around you, having a biblical foundation is top priority. Today's godly men also need a deep understanding of our country. They need to be acquainted with the men who created the bedrock of our government and need to grasp the principles on which it was built. That begins with solid knowledge of American history.

The Book of Deuteronomy is a very good example of what I mean. Moses wrote all but the last portion, which is about his death. In Deuteronomy, Moses taught the Israelites about the history of their exodus from Egypt and their trek in the desert for forty years, about how God provided for them and rebuked them during their rebellious periods.

Remember, the majority of these Jewish clans were not around when the Red Sea parted, or when Moses came down from Mount Sinai with the two tablets. Caleb and Joshua, and, of course, Moses, but few others survived the forty years of wandering in the Negev. Moses wanted to ensure the current generation of Israelites was fully aware of their history and would be able to pass that on to their descendants. An awareness of history was critical to the future of the Jewish clans, and Moses assumed the role of instructor to share that history with those who would pass it on to the next generation.

Remembering American history

Why are Americans losing pride in being American? Why is it over 50 percent of millennials—just over 60 percent in a recent survey— are not proud of their American heritage? Why is that? Perhaps it's because they haven't learned their history or were taught revised history. I believe there has been a deliberate effort by liberal educators to not teach factual American history or government in our public schools. And whatever history is being taught is either untrue or is presented in a manner that in no way encourages students to be proud of our past or our form of government.

For example, you'll hear university professors claim, because America dropped the bombs on Hiroshima and Nagasaki during World War II, our country is "on the wrong side of history."

As I mentioned in the last chapter, President Harry Truman chose to drop those bombs to end the bloodbath going on in World War II's Pacific Theater and to save a million or more lives, both American and Japanese. And how about the fact American forces also liberated two continents and rescued untold millions from the tyranny of Nazi Germany and Imperial Japan? Shouldn't we be both proud and grateful? The sacrifices made by so many Americans, to preserve liberty for countries around the globe, should give every American a right to be gratified.

Yet what our youth experience, in a lot of public schools, is a focus on the fact that many of the founders were slave owners. Of course, we should acknowledge that unpleasant flaw in the character of those men, but we should simultaneously give them enormous credit for creating a nation that has done more for the world—as a whole—than any other nation in history.

I believe we have a generation of people who are not proud of their country because they don't know the first thing about what America is all about. Why is history so important? Because if you don't understand where you come from, you can be led into Marxism, atheism, and other aberrant things—at least aberrant to me. That's what happens when you don't know how we got here. My friend Stu Weber quotes a proverb, "If you dwell in the past, you lose an eye. If you forget the past, you lose both eyes."

Bringing up children isn't just about providing for them or teaching them to be respectful, truthful, and obedient. The first, and most important, lessons they need to learn are about knowing God, walking with Him, and living their lives according to the principles in His word. But I also believe—especially in the present climate of today's world—our sons and daughters need to know the history of the United States. The first instructor to introduce the great stories of American history will probably be Dad or Grandpa. That's you and me.

But those lessons don't necessarily stop at the family's front door. It's important for a man, whether he's the CEO of a corporation, a construction worker, a pastor, or a law enforcement officer—no matter what he does for a living—to speak to those he employs, or works with, or ministers to, about our country's heritage. After hearing some of the stories of America's early days and the strong faith of many of our Founding Fathers, how could any of us help but feel honored to be part of it?

Truthfully, a lot of the confusion and anger in our country today lies in the fact that our younger generations, in large part, are totally ignorant about how America began and on what principles it was founded. When I was teaching college classes, it was unbelievable how little my students knew about the country they called home. In fact, I could tell after the first night's class which students came out of a homeschool background and which ones came out of the public school system. The dividing line was always history.

If they were homeschooled, they knew their history—and particularly American history, which is a very important part of the homeschooling movement's curriculum. It's also a vital component of a complete education. Any man in a leadership role—whether in the family, or in commerce, industry, or politics—should find a way to impart that history. He should know what he's talking about and he should exude pride in being part of this great country.

We've talked about knowing God ourselves and knowing about Him. We'll talk more about that in the chapters that follow, but do we remember how many of our Founding Fathers were truly God-fearing men? Many of them were deeply Christian in their beliefs, or at least profoundly formed by the faith of their fathers.

Think about this, for example, in light of some of today's atheistic political rants:

> God, who gave us life, gave us liberty. Can the liberties of a nation be secure when we have removed a conviction that these liberties are the gift of God? Indeed, I tremble for my country when I reflect that God is just, that His justice cannot sleep forever.[6]

These are the words of Thomas Jefferson etched in the marble of his memorial in Washington, D.C. A brilliant thinker and the author of America's original founding document, the Declaration of Independence. Jefferson was considered by some historians to be a deist. Remember, deists believe in a "clock-maker" God who created the universe but is now hands off, so no need to pray to a God that doesn't providentially intervene in in human affairs.

Not only did Jefferson deny being a deist, but I, for one, do not concur with that view of him either, based on my personal study of the man plus the views of Mark Beliles in his book *Doubting Thomas?: The Religious Life and Legacy of Thomas Jefferson.* In his later years, as Beliles notes, Jefferson privately assumed more Unitarian beliefs. Jefferson doubted the veracity of Scriptural claims in the Gospels and Epistles about the deity of Jesus, but that did nothing to curb his public support for Trinitarian Christian worship, preachers, publications, and missionary efforts.[7] In any case, judging simply from Jefferson's statements found on his memorial, he certainly understood that the fear of God is the beginning of wisdom. And he also seemed to realize God's justice wasn't something to be taken lightly.

On Thanksgiving Day in 1986, President Ronald Reagan paid tribute to our first President, George Washington, perhaps America's most beloved hero. Reagan said:

> One of the most inspiring portrayals of American history is that of George Washington on his knees in the snow at Valley Forge. That moving image personifies and testifies to our Founders' dependence upon Divine Providence during the darkest hours of our Revolutionary struggle. It was then—when our mettle as a nation was tested most severely—that the Sovereign and Judge of nations heard our plea and came to our assistance in the form of aid from France. Thereupon General Washington immediately called for a special day of thanksgiving among his troops.[8]

In October 1789, Washington wrote, "Whereas it is the duty of all Nations to acknowledge the providence of Almighty God, to obey His will, to be grateful for His benefits, and humbly to implore His protection and favor…[I] recommend to the People of the United States a day of public thanksgiving and prayer to be observed by acknowledging with grateful hearts the many signal favors of Almighty God, especially by affording them an opportunity peaceably to establish a form of government for their safety and happiness."[9]

These days, our national conversation—if you could call it that—involves some very loud, very angry voices. Broadcast widely across twenty-four-hour news stations, anti-American ideologues claim that any reference to God, or any support of America's Judeo-Christian tradition, should be forbidden in the public square. Some detractors openly mock Christianity. Others claim the Bible discriminates against homosexuals and so do those who read it, quote it, or preach it. Still others are openly promoting Islam or atheism—even in the halls of Congress.

Can you see why it's essential for us to embrace the faith of our nation's fathers and teach it to our children? It is absolutely true many of America's founders were fervent Christians, who wanted to build into America the same values—life, liberty, and the pursuit of happiness—God instilled in humanity. They knew first-hand those freedoms were denied to them under British rule. They wanted to create a better world, as they put it, "for ourselves and our posterity."

John Adams, the second U.S. President, was a devoted Christian. He once wrote, "The general principles on which the fathers achieved independence were...the general principles of Christianity. I will avow that I then believed, and now believe, that those general principles of Christianity are as eternal and immutable as the existence and attributes of God."[10]

If you've ever seen an image of the Declaration of Independence, you couldn't have missed John Hancock's signature. He made it big enough for all the world to see. He was just as outspoken about his faith as he was about his gratitude for America's founding. He asked people to pray "that universal happiness may be established in the world [and] that all may bow to the scepter of our Lord Jesus Christ, and the whole earth be filled with His glory."[11]

And Abraham Lincoln—what a great man he was! Just think about the fact he was self-taught. He grew up in a log cabin, and he had to sit by the fire at night to have enough light to read. I wonder if today's college graduates even know that part of his story.

Near the end of the Civil War, he wrote in a letter, "I am naturally anti-slavery. If slavery is not wrong, nothing is wrong. I cannot remember when I did not so think and feel.... Now, at the end of three years [sic] struggle the nation's condition is not what either party, or any man devised, or expected. God alone can claim it...If God now wills the removal of a great wrong, and wills also that we of the North, as well as you of the South, shall pay fairly for our complicity in that wrong, impartial history will find therein new cause to attest, and revere the justice and goodness of God."[12]

Can you see why understanding American history is so important for us as Christian men? No doubt we've all got some gaps in our knowledge about the Founding Fathers and the dramatic history that followed them, including brutal wars that both secured our land and ended the curse of slavery. There are countless books and films and documentaries that can fill in the details. I hope you'll learn more and share what you learn with others.

It bears repeating this is not just about telling old heroic stories to your immediate family. Whatever your work involves, whoever it is you talk to every day, whenever you have a chance to speak to a group—that is your sphere of influence. For example, if you're an employer and you bring new employees aboard, you invest in those people. And part of the way you can invest in them would be by helping them understand our country's history as well as the history and values of the business you represent. Every organization has a history with something noteworthy employees should know.

In the military, where I spent most of my life, we worked hard to make new members of our various combat units proud to serve in their particular unit. We did that by educating them, by sharing with them their unit's unique history. I told you before about the importance of the Ranger Creed.

I was also part of the creation of the Delta Force. We founded Delta at Fort Bragg, North Carolina, in 1978. Now, for me, looking back, our Force four decades later is amazing. If you examine the record that unit has amassed in forty years, the record of accomplishments will shock you. Many, if not most, of Delta's operations are classified. Besides being the ones to kill Abu Bakr al-Baghdadi, Delta operators have carried out some of the world's most dangerous and secretive operations—from Iran to Grenada, from Colombia to Iraq, from Afghanistan to Somalia, and far beyond. When new operators come into the Force today, it's essential for their leadership to introduce them to Delta Force's history. That history is the lineage they want to be part of, and they're proud to know they're going to keep building upon that legacy.

A good reading program is fundamental to becoming an instructor. Too often, well-meaning men get into altered history because they take snippets from websites or speeches of people who are intentionally denigrating the history of America, the military, or some other key issue in history. These American-hating yahoos are the same ones who want every American to buy the lie that the only thing we need to know about WWII is the U.S. dropped atomic bombs on Japan because we are a racist nation. If you don't know the truth, it will be difficult to set the record straight with the folks you influence.

And, if you are one of those fellows who would say to me "Well I am just not much of a reader," my response is, "Yeah, I understand that, but you need to change and try to get into it." If computer games are robbing you of reading time, just stop that foolish nonsense. Get books on tape and listen while driving if you have to. And, by the way, I have Attention Deficit Disorder (ADD), so I understand the problems we ADD types have with staying focused. But trust me—I know from experience you can get better at it as you read more.

Building a noble legacy

Closer to home and sooner rather than later, every man needs to ask himself, "What is my legacy going to be? How do I want people to remember me? How can I create the legacy I want to leave behind me?"

If you look for a definition of "legacy" in the dictionary, it will tell you something about a financial inheritance; a legacy is defined as "an amount of money or property left to someone in a will."

That's not what we're talking about here. I'm interested in another kind of legacy.

Of course, we don't have a legacy until we're dead and gone. But, up until then, we're establishing a history that will culminate in our legacy. In the meantime, we need to think about where we go, who we go with, what we say and do, and why those things matter, day in and day out. Ask yourself these questions.

For what will you be best remembered? Or put another way, what stories will be told about you when you're gone?

If you're an artist, you might think of your most beautiful painting as your legacy. If you're a writer, maybe you'll try to leave behind a best seller with your name on the cover. If you're a soldier, you might keep track of the stripes and medals you've earned. If you're a businessman, your legacy may be the story of how you built your business from next to nothing and turned it into an empire.

There's an enormous sporting goods store in Springfield, Missouri, that I visited not so long ago. I'm guessing that every serious sportsman knows about Bass Pro Shops—it's one of the best-known sporting goods chains in North America. And, since I'm known to be an avid hunter and fisherman, while I was in Missouri speaking at a conference, my hosts took me to the new Bass Pro Museum.

Johnny Morris is the founder and CEO of Bass Pro. Even as a small boy, Johnny was an avid angler, and when he got a little older, he wanted to try his hand at selling fishing gear. His father let him set up shop in an eight-square-foot area in the back of his local convenience and liquor store. Johnny proceeded to start selling fishing lures and tackle.

Eight square feet in that little store, and today young Johnny Morris's boyhood dream has turned into one of the largest sporting goods centers in the world. In 2019, Bass Pro shops had forty thousand employees. They had one hundred and fifty stores with two hundred million visitors. Their annual revenue is eight billion dollars.

To create the Bass Pro Museum, Johnny Morris reassembled a portion of his father's old store, including pieces of the roof and interior. He recycled those pieces from the past to create a memorial to his father, who made it possible for him to pursue his childhood dream. His museum also allows people to see for themselves an incredible fulfillment of the American dream.

His father bequeathed him the opportunity, and now the son hopes to inspire and encourage other young visionaries to believe that their dreams really are achievable. The success story of Bass Pro Shops is Johnny Morris's legacy.

As for me—and I think the same is true with most men, at least those who have children—my legacy will be whatever instruction and guidance I've provided for my sons and daughters and the impact I've had on their lives. A lot of people won't remember I had a thirty-six-year military career. They won't know I worked with the Family Research Council or spoke at hundreds of churches and conferences. They will know me almost entirely through the character of my children.

That legacy is one I can be proud of.

What about you? How can you begin now to build the legacy you'll leave behind in the future? It's important to give some thought to that. Because no matter how good our intentions are, if we deviate from the right path, our legacy could be exactly the opposite of what we hoped for.

Think for a moment about Bill Clinton. People naturally like him—he has a pleasant personality. And if he hadn't gotten involved with Monica Lewinsky—the first of several scandals we've heard about—he might well have been remembered as one of America's most successful presidents. I didn't vote for him, and I'm not a big supporter of his, but he was an effective president.

However, sexual temptations got the best of Bill Clinton. What are people going to remember about him? Probably that he was a womanizer in the White House. And that reality has ruined his chances for a great legacy. In fact, I think in the eyes of historians, it's done irreparable damage.

He's not the only one. I think many men are far too concerned with living for today than giving serious thought to tomorrow. Temptation isn't hard to find, as the recent "Me Too" testimonies have revealed. In fact, one of the biggest problems in American society is a continuing sexual revolution—more about that in the next chapter.

We've all heard the story, and more than once: a man leaves his family because he's run into some woman who has "stolen his heart." No, she hasn't "stolen" your heart, knucklehead—she's stolen your hormones, but certainly not your heart!

Too often that man leaves his family so he can live with this new woman. Does he understand he's never going to be the same man he once was in the eyes of his children or ex-wife? They may accept him, they may forgive him, they may be good to him, but he's never going to recover the respect he's lost in their hearts.

And of course, sex isn't the only pitfall that can ruin a man's legacy.

A guy in the projects gets busted for drug dealing. He'll serve jail time.

An investment advisor starts cutting corners with his clients' money, and winds up stealing hundreds of thousands of dollars. He's served with a warrant for grand larceny, not to mention tax evasion. Federal prison is in his future.

Another man loses one job after another because he refuses to follow the instructions he's been given by his supervisors. He's quite sure he knows a lot more than they do, but the one thing he never learned was how to respect authority. Now he's unemployed, broke, and bitter.

Meanwhile, there's a different kind of man who also has to face a difficult future. He got blown up by an IED on some dirt road in Afghanistan. He's going to be disabled for life. It won't be easy for him to carry on, but he knows he was doing his part for his country and his fellow soldiers. He had every reason to be right where he was, in the line of fire.

He gave up part of himself for a transcendent cause, and that's a legacy he can be proud of.

Loving, providing for, and instructing our children is a parent's transcendent cause. For Johnny Morris, reaching for success became his transcendent cause. So is serving our country and being willing to take a bullet—or an IED—for the men fighting next to you.

There's an even higher calling. The Bible sums it up in just a few words, "The fear of the Lord is the beginning of knowledge, but fools despise wisdom and instruction" (Prov. 1:7 [KJV]).

What does it mean to "fear the Lord?" It means to hold Him in awe, to understand He is sovereign and has no equal.

Those of us who have chosen to be providers and instructors to our families and beyond shouldn't be surprised if, now and then, somebody turns his back on what we have to say to him. That can be discouraging and even humiliating. If and when it happens, it's good to remember anyone who refuses to listen to wisdom or to receive instruction, according to the Bible, is a fool.

But in choosing to fear and honor the Lord, and by becoming the providers and instructors we're intended to be, we're doing our part in honoring the greatest transcendent cause in the world. In the next chapter, we'll take a look at another aspect of the responsibility that belongs to every man: being a defender.

In all these things, as we continue to grow into the kind of men we're called to be in today's world, we can rest assured our legacy will be both honorable and everlasting.

MAN AS AN INSTRUCTOR—
A WORD FOR WOMEN

In most homes, if mom is home during the day, she does much of the teaching when it comes to educating small children. She spends more time with the kids than Dad does, especially in the early years, and she's continually instructing them and answering their (often endless!) questions all day long. Later, in the following years, many, if not most, elementary school classrooms are taught by women. Of course, the same is frequently true with homeschooling.

That means the voice of knowledge and information in the family may primarily be a female one. In fact, even Alexa—the robotic, know-it-all answer machine—speaks with a woman's voice.

When Dad comes home from work, he may be ready to take a serious break after a long, hard day. He's more than happy to tune into Monday Night Football after dinner, or to pursue some other diversion that sidetracks him from his daily responsibilities.

In the course of this, it's sometimes easy for men to leave the teaching—and the search for information that invites it—to the woman of the house. "Ask your mom!" can become the answer of choice.

Naturally there are men who thrive on knowing and explaining—whether they are specialized experts or are just guys who read a lot and like to share their thoughts. But there's a point when a well-informed male perspective, on some issues, can provide an essential voice to inform and instruct his wife and family.

Finally, as the old saying goes, "The family that prays together stays together." A family time of Bible stories, learning memory verses, and prayer is precious with small children. When Dad leads these conversations as the kids grow toward puberty and into young adulthood, they are gifted with a lifelong role model. Listening to his reflections and instructions on all kinds of serious topics in light of the Bible's perspective is time well spent. George Barna, the renowned researcher and author, says a child's worldview is set in concrete by the age of thirteen.[13] So, please, encourage your man to take on the role of instructor if he is deficient in that area. Help him and show him how the family benefits from him performing his duties as an instructor.

Man as an Instructor—
Discussion Questions

1. As a founding member of the first U.S. Ranger battalion, General Boykin relayed how his unit commander recited their history, going back to World War II. How important is it to pass on a sense of history and heritage, that we are a part of something more important, and larger than we are, as individuals? What steps could you take toward making that a reality with your family or your colleagues?

2. As the resident teacher for your family, how important is it to be armed with solid, reliable information? In the age of "fake news," truth is difficult to discern. There are precious few one-stop shops that offer common sense, let alone biblical perspectives. Develop a game plan for gathering reliable information and pray for the timing to communicate it, hopefully with some biblical wisdom to match.

3. How do you identify yourself? Pray about it, think it through, then write it down as it comes to you. Any change needed in the list with regards to priority?

4. As the instructor, you need to make sure you can teach the Bible, but in order to do this, you must first understand it yourself. On a scale of one to ten, how would you rate your grasp of basic biblical truths and the ability to communicate them? If needed,

there are plenty of good commentaries and online helps. If you don't know where to start, talk to a pastor or fellow Christian to get some solid suggestions.

5. What are some ways biblical faith and values are in conflict with the culture? How can you communicate that information to your family in a natural way?

6. What are some practical ways you can model and instill biblical masculinity in the males in your family and circle of relationships?

7. As you read this chapter, was your image of Jesus challenged? In what way?

8. Any man in a leadership role should find a way to impart history to others, not only biblical history, but our American history. How can you use your influence to teach others about the greatness of America, our godly heritage, and our heroes? There are precious few reliable sources for this vital information, but a good place to start is by reading biographies of Founding Fathers and great Americans.

9. In this chapter, we discussed building a noble legacy. How do you want people to remember you? How can you create the legacy you want to leave behind you? How can you begin to build that legacy now?

10. No matter how good our intentions are, if we deviate from the right path, our legacy could be exactly the opposite of what we hoped for. What can you do to make sure you don't deviate from the right path? In other words, what temptations do you struggle with that could ruin your legacy, and how can you make sure that doesn't happen?

CHAPTER THREE

MAN AS A DEFENDER

A father...shields his family members from anything that could harm or invade his wife and children. He is often the one that family members come to when they feel anxious or threatened. If another man tries to abuse or insult his wife, her husband defends her honor and her body with his life, if necessary. It is his responsibility to see that the house is safe at night and that the children come home at a reasonable time. Each member of the family feels a little more secure because he is there.

—James Dobson[14]

Defend the weak and the fatherless; uphold the cause
of the poor and the oppressed. Rescue the weak and the
needy; deliver them from the hand of the wicked.

—Psalm 82:3–4 (NIV)

J ust before Thanksgiving in 2017, I was driving down the high-way just north of Richmond. I was cruising along I-95 at about seventy-five miles an hour when I saw a woman on the side of the road getting roughed up by a man. Alongside what appeared to be his car, I saw a man holding onto this woman by her hair. He was swinging her around in a circle and as I went by, he slammed her on the ground and kicked her. Then he sat on top of her and started punching.

I immediately pulled off the highway, steering in ahead of the two other cars between my and the assailant's vehicle. Both of those drivers were women, and it looked like they were calling 911. Once I stopped, I reached over and grabbed my Kimber 1911 forty-five-caliber pistol, and I started to run along the edge of the highway to reach the assailant to stop him.

Of course, my mind was going at warp speed. *Do I shoot the guy, or do I try to knock him out with my pistol? What am I gonna do?* Thoughts were flying through my head faster than I could run.

My conclusion: I could live with standing before a judge, but I couldn't live with letting that thug kill the woman—and it looked very much like that's what he was trying to do. So, right before I reached him, I raised my pistol. When he saw my gun, he scrambled off the woman. She struggled to her feet, clearly in a lot of pain, and moved slowly around the car to get out of his reach.

With the pistol pointed at his face, I backed him up against the car.

"What are you gonna' do with that gun?" he asked. He was no fool, and he realized the seriousness of the situation as he looked down the barrel of a forty-five-caliber pistol.

"I'm gonna' shoot you if you touch that woman again." By then we both knew I would use it if he made the wrong move.

Of course, I'm thinking, the only thing people driving down I-95 are going to remember is this white man jacking a round in the chamber of a pistol as he's running toward a black man.

Fortunately, the attacker's attitude changed quickly—just as a woman driving a Department of Transportation vehicle screeched to a halt. She had a badge, and I said to myself, "Here we go. They're going to arrest me now, watch this…"

But she didn't. Instead she said, "You hold him there while I check on her."

I stood right where I was and held the pistol on him. Apparently, the transportation officer already received a full report, probably from one of the women who called 911.

Then, while I was standing there holding the gun on the guy and the transportation officer was checking on the woman, two Virginia State Police pulled up.

I thought, "Well, this is it for sure."

They walked over to me. I shoved my pistol into my belt, and said, "I have a concealed carry." One of them said, "Oh yeah, that's fine. Tell me what you saw here."

And that was the end of it—I filled them in on what happened and never heard from them again.

The point was, I couldn't drive by and not do something about what was going on—I *had* to do something to stop it. First of all, I'm a man. Secondly, somebody had to help that woman, or her abuser was probably going to kill her. Turned out he had already broken her ribs. Thirdly, why do I have a concealed carry permit if not for that kind of situation? To stop a woman from possibly being killed, and certainly being battered.

Bystander effect

In this chapter I'm going to be talking about the fact that a man is meant to be a *Defender*, a protector—not just of family and next of kin. Of all, as the Bible says, including the poor, oppressed, the weak, and the needy.

That story also illustrates the importance of never walking past an event—particularly one involving a woman being mistreated in any way—because today that's a common thing. Incredibly, even while girls or women get raped or otherwise assaulted in public places, people just walk right on by and don't do anything. Grown men turn their heads away, check their phones, and do nothing.

Just keep this in mind—there are worse things that can happen to you than getting your ass kicked for trying to do the right thing.

Nowadays, this practice of doing nothing while someone else suffers even has a name, according to *Psychology Today* magazine. It's called the "bystander effect," and it occurs "when the presence of others discourages an individual from intervening in an emergency situation."

> Social psychologists Bibb Latané and John Darley popularized the concept following the infamous 1964 Kitty Genovese murder in New York City. As Genovese was stabbed to death outside her apartment, neighbors failed to step in to assist or call the police. Latané and Darley attributed the bystander effect to the perceived *diffusion of responsibility* (onlookers are less likely to intervene if there are other witnesses who seem likely to do so) and social influence (individuals monitor the behavior of those around them to determine how to act)."[15]

This kind of uncaring detachment from reality really is a problem today—now and then you'll see a video of an incident like that on YouTube. It is literally unbelievable to me. As far as I'm concerned, a man who would walk past that sort of thing is not a man at all. At the very least, he's clearly not fulfilling the role of a man as a defender.

What if you were an onlooker in a situation like that? There might be four or five abusers and just one of you, but you've still got to get involved in whatever way you can. I don't advocate for wannabe heroes who go out and play the martyr, saying "Kill me and leave her alone." What I do advocate for is to step forward and make it very clear you are taking action—some kind of action, like calling the police. Don't walk down the street, go around the corner, and call for help. If you're on the scene at a time like that, your very presence may be a deterrent. Your being there may stop the troublemakers from completing whatever it is they're trying to do, which may be raping a female, or mugging her, or slapping her around.

If you walk on by, you're just wrong. But men today do just that in so many cases because it is safer and easier to take the attitude that it is none of their business. Wrong, just wrong!

This idea of being a defender isn't just about being protective of your family or your wife or your children—although that's certainly part of it. It's really about you being a man. And you're probably going to have more than a few opportunities to take action, just by living in today's messed up world, particularly if you're in an urban area.

It's happened to me more than once. One night, as I got out of my car in the parking lot of my townhouse in Alexandria, Virginia, I heard a man yelling at a woman. By then I was out of my car. I watched as she yelled something back at him and he walked over and smacked her. I stepped back to my vehicle and grabbed a tire knocker and a pistol. Then I headed toward the couple with the pistol in one hand and the tire knocker in the other.

I guess the man in question must have realized I wasn't going to allow him to hit her again, so he took off.

That's the reason we have to be prepared, as the Bible puts it, "in season and out of season," for situations where this kind of thing happens. Maybe you need to start thinking, "What would I do? How would I deal with it?"

If you're like me, you'll make sure you're armed. Because today you can't afford not to be armed if you're going to be out and about, mixing with society. I travel all around this United States—I'm in good places and I'm in bad places. I don't go into bad places unless I have some way to defend myself.

Now some of you may think I am advocating for everyone to carry a weapon and you may be a "gun control" advocate. Well, you are absolutely right about me—I do advocate everyone owning, and knowing how to operate, a weapon.

Frankly, I don't think our subject matter here is only a question of *who* a man should protect; it's also a question of *what*. A man has a responsibility to protect that which he holds dear, and those things don't always come in the form of other humans.

I spent thirty-six plus years in the uniform of the U.S. Army and my great passion was feeling a sense of accomplishment in protecting the most precious document outside of the Bible and that's the Constitution of the United States. I had a transcendent cause and I think many—if not most—of those who serve in the military believe they're doing their part to protect their nation. The majority of law enforcement personnel are men and it also gives them a sense of accomplishment to know they have been in a role of protecting and defending the people for whom they're responsible.

What else does a man protect and defend? He defends the values he holds dear. How about the value of the First Amendment? "Congress shall make no laws respecting an establishment of religion or prohibiting the free exercise thereof."

A man of faith believes his ability to exercise his faith is essential to him, his family, and his culture. So, he defends that freedom by being willing to stand up for it. That's part of being a defender— being willing to take a stand. Psalm 94:16 (NIV) says, "Who will rise up for me against the wicked? Who will take a stand for me against evildoers?" God is talking to believers in this verse. He is exhorting us to stand against evil. I think it's protecting and defending when you rise up against the kind of evil that is increasingly encroaching on our society.

Assaults against our families

The American family unit is under attack in our present day. We may not have to defend our loved ones physically—at least not yet—but dangerous strategies are putting us all in the line of fire ideologically, and legally. This is the result of seditious organizations, including the concerted efforts of "progressive" feminists, many of whom are deeply influenced by Marxism.

There's nothing new under the sun. For example, in the 1960s, a radical group—some of whom were among the founders of NOW, the National Organization of Women—launched a serious campaign seeking to undermine traditional family roles. Their purpose was articulated by pioneering feminist leader Kate Millett.

In 2014, Kate's sister Mallory Millett described in *FrontPage Magazine* what she witnessed as a young divorcee, during one of her sister's subversive gatherings. The women in attendance performed a call-and-response Marxist chant:

> "Why are we here today?" she [Kate Millett] asked.
>
> "To make revolution," they answered in unison.
>
> "What kind of revolution?" she replied.
>
> "The Cultural Revolution," they chanted.
>
> "And how do we make Cultural Revolution?" she demanded.
>
> "By destroying the American family!" they answered.
>
> "How do we destroy the family?" she came back.
>
> "By destroying the American Patriarch," they cried exuberantly.
>
> "And how do we destroy the American Patriarch?" she replied.
>
> "By taking away his power!"
>
> "How do we destroy his power?"
>
> "By destroying monogamy!" they shouted.
>
> "How do we destroy monogamy?"
>
> "By promoting promiscuity, eroticism, prostitution and homosexuality!" they resounded.

Mallory Millet went on to say, "They proceeded with a long discussion on how to advance these goals by establishing The National Organization of Women. It was clear they desired nothing less than the utter deconstruction of Western society. The upshot was the only way to do this was to invade every American institution. Everyone must be permeated with The Revolution; the media, the educational system, universities, high schools, K-12, school boards, etc. Then, the judiciary, the legislatures, the executive branches, and even the library system."[16]

It bears repeating that the target of this movement was, and is, the American family. The trophy of their effort is the downfall of the "American Patriarch," also known as Dad. That's me. And that's you if you have kids or ever hope to. These activists' primary weaponry is sexual—they are promoting promiscuity, eroticism, prostitution, and homosexuality.

Defending against pornography

It looks to me like these women have been very successful in their efforts. How can we defend ourselves against them? The tactics they declared four decades ago are what today's men need to confront and destroy. Typically, this battleground doesn't yet involve the need for physical defenses. But the weaponry being used against us can do massive harm to body, soul, and spirit.

As defenders, we need to recognize that much of the evil presently infecting this country is on the internet. Pornography is this evil's primary manifestation and it is destroying families. I recently talked to a pastor in Michigan while I was speaking at a Christian conference. He told me pornography is such a huge problem in the church today that on Sunday morning, instead of having everybody listening to him preach, he's started up a new program for men to attend in another part of the church. It's all about helping men understand the dangers of pornography and how to tear themselves away from it. Pornography is more than temporarily exciting; it is addictive. The body's response to sexual pleasure releases endorphins and other hormones, which feel like a pleasurable drug rush.

Researcher and renowned speaker Josh McDowell says, "Most people don't realize what's happening with pornography. Basically, there's [sic] two types of men in the evangelical church—those that watch pornography and those that lie." He says porn among church-goers is "epidemic."

He explains, "At least 78.8 percent of all men that attend evangelical churches watch pornography. Probably 80 percent of all evangelical youth pastors also watch pornography, and now, the greatest increase is among women and young ladies. It's killing us. 64 percent of all Christian families have an acute problem with pornography."

McDowell goes on to say:

> No parents can protect their child from seeing pornography. Any mother right now will probably say, 'Oh no, I pray over my child', or 'I home school and so therefore I can protect my child.' When I

hear this, I look that mother right in the eye and say, 'You will lose your child. *You cannot protect your child from seeing pornography!* They will see it. What you must do is, as a responsible mother and father, is *prepare* your child for the first time they will see it, and it will probably be before eight years of age in Christian homes. In fact, in many Christian homes, it's probably four to six years old when they first come across pornography.

Of course, one big problem regarding porn in the family is Dad is going to have a very hard time warning his son or daughter about pornography when he's secretly hooked on it himself. Come on guys, you are the defenders. Defend those kids from one of the most addictive and damaging things in our society.

To make matters worse, some Christian men don't see defending their families, friends, or colleagues against such vile images, ideas, and behavior as something they should be doing. "They're just kids going through the hormone zone" or "They just need to get it out of their system," some fathers tell themselves. They don't see pushing back against this evil intrusion as their responsibility, even though that's exactly what the Bible instructs us to do.

It bears repeating: "Who will rise up for me against the wicked? Who will take a stand for me against evildoers?"

A man is called to be the defender of godly values—those things he holds dear. That means he is willing to stand and be heard, prepared to engage in activities that help protect and defend those values. That doesn't mean you have to be in uniform—law enforcement or military. It means, as a man, you are the one who has to stand against the evil threatening us all. If you are addicted to porn or even if you occasionally watch it, my advice is to get help. There are several organizations that help men. One of the best is Josh McDowell Ministry. Go to his website and its section on porn, https://www. josh.org/resources/sex-relationships/. It will be worth it.

The hidden dangers of gaming

There's another behavior I'd like to see men looking at more closely, and that's computer gaming. Children born in the 1980s were the first generation with access to vivid, realistic first-person shooter games. The Columbine, Colorado, killers Dylan Klebold and Eric Harris emerged from that generation and their horrifying 1999 mass murder marked the beginning of the school shooting epidemic. Violent video games give boys the adrenaline rush of war without the camaraderie of men fighting alongside them. And, needless to say, any goal or purpose or transcendent cause is totally absent. This is another issue in our society that demands the attention of men as defenders to eliminate the terrible consequences of gaming.

I'd like to see a study on the correlation between some of our mass school shootings and whether the murderers were gamers. I've seen shocking images on some games—all you have to do is spend thirty seconds looking at them and you can see they're right out of the pit of hell. That's not to say every computer/console game is harmful or even dangerous, but some of them truly are. I think it's just another angle Satan uses to enter our minds, create confusion, and draw us and our children and grandchildren into something very harmful.

And it's not just warfare games. There are also men who sit in front of a screen completely immersed in role-playing games. Before long they begin to take on the personality or the character whose "role" they're playing; they take on the persona of the character they've "become." In this case, I'm talking about both violence and demonism. The violent portion is obvious. How such activity can affect you spiritually and how it might well give the enemy of your soul a foothold in your life is somewhat obscure, but very real.

Then there is the issue of online gambling. Fantasy football, poker, and other games of chance are a huge problem for many men today and, like gaming, have distracted so many fathers who spend inordinate amounts of time at the computer screen instead of with the family.

We've got to remember that Satan wasn't created in Hollywood. He's real; he's a fallen angel. We need to be very careful we don't downplay the notion Satan is real. As Peter says, "Be alert and of sober mind. Your enemy, the devil, prowls around like a roaring lion looking for someone to devour" (1 Pet. 5:8 [NIV]). We need to understand we're his prime targets.

It's important for us to realize if we're men who are called by God, we're targeted even more than our spouses or our children. As we've seen in the feminist/Marxist declaration I quoted before, if the wicked spirits of the age can bring us down, they've scored a big success. We are men—and yes, we are "patriarchs"—who are God-ordained spiritual heads of houses and leaders in our communities.

It reminds me of something American soldiers and marines learned during the Vietnam War. The Viet Cong, our enemies, were always trying to shoot the guy with the radio. Why? Because in most cases he was the platoon leader. That's the head of the snake—take that one man down and you throw everything into confusion. As a man, I hope you'll recognize Satan and his minions are coming after you. And he's after you in ways you haven't even imagined.

"Run to the sounds of gunfire and the smell of cordite"

Of course, the Bible also encourages us with, "where sin increased, grace increased all the more" (Rom. 5:20 [NIV]). And in a couple of these recent school shootings, there have been young, courageous students who have run toward the shooter's gun and not away from it, even though they were never trained to react that way. I was so impressed to see that! It was something spiritual. One young man, whose funeral was partially televised, died running directly into the mass murderer's gun. What incredible courage. I would also point out this action represents the masculine instinct we should all hope we have.

Contrast that to the 1999 shooting in Columbine, Colorado, I referred to earlier. As Klebold and Harris were killing children inside the school, the police were lined up outside doing nothing. Watch a video of that day and you will see what I am talking about.

The same thing happened on February 14, 2018 at Parkland High in Florida. Nikolas Cruz killed seventeen students with his weapons, while the sheriff's deputy, Scot Peterson, hid outside and made no effort to charge the shooter and bring the situation to an end. In June 2019, Deputy Peterson was convicted of child neglect under a Florida statute. Well, he should have been in my view. A man cannot stand by and let that happen.

Once again, what does a man do in these situations? He runs toward the guns, not away from them. Men must run to the sound of the cannons because that's where the action is and it is also where a man belongs. And no, I am not advocating suicide, but there are some evils we, as men, must stop, even at the risk of our own lives.

In a similar situation, there was a gunman in a small rural church in Sutherland Springs, Texas, who started shooting worshippers one Sunday morning. Down the street about a hundred and fifty yards lived a man named Stephen Willeford. Upon hearing the shots, Willeford grabbed his AR-15 and ran to the sound of the gunfire. Mr. Willeford killed the gunman in front of the church and saved an untold number of lives because he acted like a man, he played the role of a man, and he measured up as a man. Makes me wonder—are all the real men in this country living in rural Texas or do we have more men like Stephen Willeford elsewhere? I hope and pray it is the latter.

You can't watch evil being perpetrated and just walk by, thinking "I don't want to get involved." A real problem in our country today is we've become comfortable telling ourselves "Well, this isn't any of my business." No, wrong. It *is* your business. It's your business if a woman is being slapped around or some other abuse is taking place. I think that's also true when you see a child being abused or neglected.

Honestly, I don't even care if it's a parent doing it. If a child is being harmed in a physical way, as far as I'm concerned, I've got to step in and put a stop to that. We've all seen episodes like that some place or another. If we're going to be godly men, we have to defend the values we cherish as well as protect people who are unable to defend or protect themselves. As men, we have a unique responsibility to intervene and do the best we can to put a stop to an abusive, dangerous, or threatening situation.

Defending the defenseless

If we're supposed to be concerned about child abuse, what about the killing of unborn babies? As men, we need to face the facts about what's happening in America. That's a difficult thing for more than a few men to do, because in some cases some men are doing what the Bible has clearly told us not to do—pretending everything is fine and thereby calling good evil and evil good. It's time we confronted this cold, hard fact—*there is evil in the land.*

From my perspective, the most fundamental right is the right to life. And we are killing *babies*. We've killed sixty million that we know about. It continues, although we're starting to see some healthy changes taking place. I hope and pray that trend continues.

The question is, if a man is called to be a defender, is he supposed to get engaged in this whole issue of Right to Life? Should he try to deal with the question of whether life begins at conception? My answer is yes. There is no one more helpless, no one more innocent, than an unborn baby, moving around in that embryonic sac and totally dependent on the mother. They are the most vulnerable of all humankind.

Men ought to have a deep passion for wanting to protect and defend those innocent babies, just as a matter of principle. And not just his own offspring—I'm talking about babies in general. But in practical terms, how does a man put his protective instincts into practice? To begin with, when it comes to abortion issues, I think men should get very engaged in their church and local community. Why do I say that? Because it is our state legislatures that make the laws governing abortion in each of our fifty states. The problem is that they never hear from the right people.

For example, in your state you may have a Right to Life organization working hard to rectify this kind of violence against the unborn. But what are *you* doing? Are you engaged in protecting infants whose lives are going to be taken in your state? You need to seek out one of those organizations. Maybe a crisis pregnancy center in your community needs volunteers. Or you could talk to your pastor or some other knowledgeable person—one who is able to suggest some constructive ways you can get engaged in the issue.

Most men will say, "I'm one hundred percent pro-life," but when you ask, "How are you trying to stop abortion?" they look back at you with a blank stare. That's because they're not doing a thing about it. Yes, you can write a check to help fund these organizations trying to stop abortion, but there are also other ways to get involved.

Where do you live? What are the laws in your state? You need to know what your state legislature is doing. We all need to know what's up for a vote in our home states. If we don't get involved, we're going to wind up just like New York, where Governor Andrew Cuomo signed one of the most radical abortion laws in the country, making abortion legal right up until the moment of birth.[17] Governor Cuomo and the legislature then cheered like they'd won the Super Bowl, even lighting up the One World Trade Center! Even after a baby is born, the law allows for a discussion between the doctor and mother to see whether the baby is going to be allowed to live. That, my friends, is murder.

And, just to put it in perspective, think about the fact Governor Cuomo recently signed a law prohibiting the declawing of cats statewide in New York. They frown on causing cats pain and celebrate the killing of preborn babies!

Please read Isaiah 5:20—it is a warning about calling good evil and evil good.

We are so upside down, in our society, on our priorities in life. What matters to you? What do you hold dear? Defend that which you care about and don't compromise because your actions offend someone. Show me anything that does not offend somebody. In any case, according to His Word, you are certainly not offending God when you act like a man.

When a bill regarding abortion goes to a vote before your state lawmakers, pick up the phone and call your local representative. Let them know what you believe and what you think about the bill in question. In making that call, or in writing a check, or in otherwise speaking out, you're performing your role as a defender. You may have a passion for golf and fishing. I hope you'll take that same kind of passion and put it into practice when it comes to protecting the unborn. We all need to put our passions into action.

One of the things that frustrates me is when men say, "I don't even watch the news anymore because it's too depressing." I don't even know how to respond to that. Yes, it's depressing, which is exactly why you need to know what's going on.

But once you've decided to start paying attention, let me offer a word to the wise; stay away from conspiracy theories. There are some bloggers, some websites, and some prominent personalities out there who are into all kinds of weird ideas and are drawing strange conclusions. Along similar lines, if you haven't figured it out yet, the dark side of our culture will feed you lies just so you'll make a fool of yourself repeating them. In any case, don't tune out! We all need to know what's going on in this country and there are plenty of credible sources of information available. It takes a little diligence to confirm what is true and is well worth the effort for you, your family, and friends.

If you're a man, don't forget for a minute you're meant to be a defender of those who can't defend themselves. That's why you can't turn away, stand aside, or choose to watch from afar what's happening and do nothing about it. You, as a man, came out of the womb called to be a warrior. In fact, Exodus 15:3 (NIV) makes it very clear, "The Lord is a warrior; the Lord is his name." Stop and think about that. I think we just skip over that as a metaphor. But no, it's not a metaphor. It says the Lord is a *warrior*, and we know we are made in His image.

Unfortunately, American society today is trying very hard to convince us otherwise. We're being bombarded with the message, masculinity is "toxic," and especially when it is demonstrated according to biblical authority. But the reality is far different. Because of the specific way God created us, as males, we're on the right track toward becoming warriors ourselves, if we choose to follow the path God has mapped out for us.

It bears repeating—a man is defender of any person who needs to be protected. That's why a man who walks past someone who's being abused or threatened and does nothing about it is dead wrong. I hope that man looks in the mirror when he shaves the next morning and sees he is *disgusting* because he didn't make the effort he should have. I'm not advocating that you should go out and sacrifice your life, but again, there are worse things than getting your backside kicked, like losing your dignity, which is far worse.

Defending our children against destructive behavior

Unfortunately, our role as protector and defender doesn't always happen outside the front door of our own homes. There are times when the head of the house and the father of the family has to step in and take defensive action in a preventative way. We have to develop the foresight to realize that if we don't act now, something going on under our own roof is about to become far worse, and perhaps even deadly, if left unaddressed. It will take a father's firm hand to turn the situation around.

A mother's love often comes to mind when we think about family ties. A mother's love for her children is an emotional, even passionate love. It manifests itself in a number of ways. One is sympathy and empathy. Another is a desire to solve the crisis of the moment. "I want us to get through this and get back to normal." The mother is the hen gathering her chicks, trying to keep them safe and protected. Thank you, Lord, for that instinct in mothers.

A father's love—a man's love—is quite different. It also involves a passionate love for his children. However, the father is the one who must love his kids enough to tell them the truth and hold them accountable. The father should be the strategic thinker with recognition of how bad choices by a son or daughter will have lifelong consequences.

One day, some years ago, I said to my fifteen-year-old son, "You can't continue to live in this house if you smoke marijuana. If you do it again, you're going to have to leave."

He did it again and I caught him.

I reminded him of what I said before. Then I told him, "Go pack up your stuff." He did. He threw some clothes and a few other items into a backpack. We got into the car in silence. I drove him to the mall, pulled up to the entrance and told him to take his belongings and get out of the car.

I said, "I love you. So, if you decide you love your family more than drugs, let me know and we'll work something out." And I drove away.

I cried all the way home, but I loved that young man enough to draw a hard line. I told myself, "If I don't take a stand and send a clear message right now, he's on the path to self-destruction."

That's an example of a father's love in contrast to a mother's love, which would more likely say, "How do I help get you out of this trouble you're in?" However, in this case, my wife was fully support-ive of the action, although her heart was breaking.

A father's love will look at the situation more strategically, seeing it from a long-range perspective. That father says, "I'm not going to tell you what you want to hear because it makes you feel good or because it will stop you from resenting me for telling it like it is. I love you enough I'm going to tell you the truth, and if it puts you off or alienates our relationship, I'm willing to pay that price. And why is that? Because the Bible says, 'You will know the truth, and the truth will set you free' (John 8:32 [NIV]). It's only a matter of time until the truth will resonate with you and not just with me."

And yes, our boy came back! I was so happy to see him. In fact, I was just as glad to see him return as his mother was. But the episode was a lesson to us all. I believe, in a biblical home, there are consequences involved in the father's love, while peacemaking efforts are evident in a mother's love. Nowadays, apart from simply addressing bad habits, it may eventually be the father's responsibility to encourage his sons and daughters to move on and find a life of their own.

We're seeing a generation of young people who continue to live with their parents, even into their thirties. Of course, I understand there are outside forces at play—higher costs of living and pricey rental payments—but the trend of "millennials living in Mom and Dad's basement" can also be a symptom of arrested development.

How can we defend our children from the danger of becoming dependent on other people—including us—rather than relying on God? We have biblical assurance our efforts will be rewarded. Proverbs 22:6 (NIV) reminds us to "start children off on the way they should go, and even when they are old, they will not turn from it."

If the Bible says it, it's true. But getting our children moving in the right direction isn't always easy. To become men who rely on God, our sons may need to be pushed out of the nest once they finish school and find a job. Our daughters may also need a nudge to move on. Being on their own enables our sons and daughters to set their feet firmly on the ground and to find direction for their future.

Take courage, men! In every circumstance, being a man who serves as a defender means demonstrating something we used to call "tough love." Besides being loving and wise parents in our own families, it includes stepping up to relieve and rescue battered women, standing up for abused children, and taking a resolute stand for the unborn.

In every case, here's the challenging bottom line; practicing tough love is—without question—toughest on the man who loves the most.

Sometimes a woman has to do a man's job

I want to finish this chapter with another story—a story about my wife, Ashley. She is the most nurturing woman I know and also one of the toughest. I am using her experience as an illustration of what happens when men don't step up and behave like the male defenders they are called to be.

I was participating in a men's conference in Redding, California, a couple of years ago when Ashley phoned me. I could tell by her voice when she said my name she was upset. Once she began to explain what just happened, I understood why. She was both shaken and furious as she told me about a trip she made to the local bank in our rural Virginia hometown.

Ashley was working in the yard as she often does, wearing her coveralls, when she suddenly remembered she needed to run to the bank and make a deposit. Because of threats made against us, she normally takes a pistol with her. But that day she decided to make a quick trip without it, since she was going to a bank—which should have been a secure destination.

As she drove into the bank parking lot and got out of the car, she watched, in amazement, as a man in full camouflage garb headed into the bank, but only after briefly pausing to pull a watch cap down, obscuring most of his face. Now most women would have immediately returned to their car and called 911 or the police, but not my wife.

Ashley went straight in behind him, determined to stop him if she could. The man took his position at the end of the line to see a teller. When two other men in the line took one look at him, they both immediately got out of line and headed for the opposite side of the bank. Ashley watched this and paused long enough to give the two cowards a long look of disgust as if to say, "Really guys? Aren't you two going to do anything?"

Even though she made her disdain for these gutless wonders very clear through her facial expression and body language, they weren't going to budge. Ashley swallowed hard and with her heart racing, stepped in line behind the man in question. She put her right hand in her coveralls pocket and covertly opened her Benchmade pocket-knife. She told me on the phone she could see her life flashing before her eyes. As her mind raced, she thought, "Looks like I'll never see my family again." But still, she wasn't willing to back down.

Instead, Ashley walked right up and confronted him. "You're not supposed to be in a bank with your face covered," she informed him. As he slowly turned, she thought, "Okay, this is it." She fingered the knife in her pocket, figuring that if he tried to assault her, she would manage to cut him at least once.

The man said, angrily, "I'm not going to be manipulated by you or anybody else."

She repeated her warning. Then all at once the man turned and quickly left the bank. After demanding the teller call the police, Ashley drove straight to the police station, recounted the story, and told them they needed to get ahold of the bank's surveillance video and find this guy.

Now it's still not clear what this yahoo had in mind. Was he up to no good? Why did he cover his face? Did he simply change his mind because Ashley confronted him? In this strange, and sad, scenario one principle was clear—when men refuse to do their job as defenders, they leave women to do it for them.

And considering the cowardliness of the two men who walked away, who knows what might have happened that day had Ashley not been there?

Man as a Defender—
A Word for Women

Today's troubled times provide plenty of reasons for women to feel uneasy or even fearful. Depending on where we live and where we go in the course of a day, real or imagined, fears can intensify our sense of vulnerability. Mothers of babies and small children are particularly sensitive to dangers and prone toward very protective actions and reactions—usually because of fear for their child's safety more than for themselves. That's the way God created us as women.

Likewise, by nature, many men also have a very protective streak—it seems to be part of most men's essential personality. Certainly, the greater the potential threat, the greater a man's determination to jump into the fray. Whatever it takes, men generally want to stand firmly between those they love and whatever is threatening them.

What about you and your home and family? What is your greatest concern about safety? Are your worries being addressed? If not, I hope you'll find a way to communicate your thoughts about security effectively, and that you'll also listen to your husband's point of view.

Often men are more concerned about security matters than women but may not talk much about them. For example, men and women don't always agree about having a home security system, or a watchdog, or keeping guns in the house. Yet these sorts of options really need to be addressed. Talking about, and listening to, one another's concerns is essential—and could be lifesaving.

And there are other dangers as well. Home invaders such as pornography, violent or occultic gaming, alcohol abuse, and drug abuse can bring painful heartbreak to an otherwise happy couple or family. Clear communication, and firmly established rules about all kinds of potential dangers, are essential and deserve the time and energy of all concerned.

Disagreements may require compromises, difficult as they are. Most of all, family prayer for protection and wisdom brings peace of mind to everyone, along with thanksgiving for God's faithful presence and promises of protection. However, if your man is on the road a lot, you need to raise the issue with him. Talk through options and offer suggestions. Don't ignore an obvious problem in your family life and in your marriage.

MAN AS A DEFENDER—
DISCUSSION QUESTIONS

1. After reading the dramatic story of the General rescuing an abused woman on a Virginia highway, ask yourself what you would have done had you witnessed such a scene playing out? Maybe you will never encounter a situation exactly like that, but have you thought about what you would do if faced with someone attacking a defenseless person?

2. Do you own a firearm? Do you know how to use it safely? If so, have you taught your wife and your children proper respect for and use of a firearm? If not, take a gun safety training course and practice using one. You never know when you may have to use it to defend yourself, your family, or someone in danger.

3. How can you apply the call to action in Psalm 94:16 (NIV), "Who will rise up for me against the wicked? Who will take a stand for me against evildoers?"

4. Pornography is destroying men, their marriages, and their families. Chances are great that you have a problem viewing it since statistics show eight out of ten males do. If so, the first step is to admit and confess it, then ask for forgiveness and help overcoming it. Now, what steps can you take to minimize your exposure to pornography and your family's exposure to it? As Josh McDowell warns, you cannot protect your child from seeing

pornography, so as a defender how can you *prepare* your child for the first time they will see it?

5. In this chapter, we discuss the hidden dangers of gaming and other forms of media. Are you aware of what your kids watch and play in the home? Do you know whether it is content they should actually be engaged with? If not, what are some steps you can take to make sure you do know what they are watching and what games they are playing?

6. What is meant by "Run to the sounds of gunfire and the smell of cordite"? List a few scenarios where you, as a man, should step up and step in to try to stop evil.

7. As a defender, it is important to defend the defenseless—that includes the unborn. What are you doing to rectify violence against the unborn? Are you engaged in protecting infants whose lives are going to be taken in your state? If not, what can you do to get involved?

8. When the Bible declares "The Lord is a Warrior" (Exod. 15:3 [NIV]) and you were made in His image and likeness (Gen. 1:26-28), what implications does that have for you as a man?

9. This chapter talks about defending our children against destructive behavior. This includes the tendency to become dependent on other people—including us—rather than relying on God. What steps can you take to make sure this doesn't happen?

10. Tough question—have you ever failed to step up as a man, and a woman had to do it instead? Resolve that you will never let it happen again because as a man, you are the defender.

CHAPTER FOUR

MAN AS A BATTLE BUDDY

Be courteous to all, but intimate with few, and let those few be well tried before you give them your confidence. True friendship is a plant of slow growth and must undergo and withstand the shocks of adversity before it is entitled to the appellation.

—George Washington

As iron sharpens iron, so one man sharpens another.

—*Proverbs 27:17 (NIV)*

I do not know, am I my brother's keeper?

—Genesis 4:9 (NIV; Cain responding
to God when asked where his brother was)

In 1994, when I turned over command of the Delta Force, I felt like my life was falling apart. It was difficult enough to leave a military unit like Delta, where I'd experienced, firsthand, some of America's most valiant and dangerous battles. I shared exhilarating victories and devastating losses with some of the nation's finest and most professional soldiers, some of whom did not come home alive, and that was devastating.

But leaving Delta wasn't the only challenge I was facing. My marriage was in trouble; my wife was struggling to cope with our move to Washington, D.C., and was spending more and more time in North Carolina on her own, or with friends. She carried an incredible weight during my time in command, as the commander's wife. The numerous funerals she attended while I lay wounded in Mogadishu took a toll on her, and before long, we were separated and eventually divorced.

As I was leaving Fort Bragg for the move to Washington, D.C., someone gave me a book called *Tender Warrior*. It was written by a well-known author and pastor named Stu Weber, who served as a Green Beret during the Vietnam War before being called into ministry. The book turned out to be one of the best gifts I've ever received. That was true for several reasons. First, and most obviously, it spoke to me during a painful period of time and strengthened my faith. It also familiarized me with the idea of mentoring young men. That experience opened an unexpected door for me and eventually led me into a new life and family.

Tender Warrior also introduced me to a true friend—the kind of friend I wish every man could have. Stu Weber, who wrote the book, has over the years become my real "battle buddy."

What do I mean by a *Battle Buddy*? When army recruits are being trained to start thinking and acting like soldiers and preparing themselves to go into combat, they are placed together in pairs by their commanding officers. The "battle buddy" nickname describes a kind of assigned best friend—assigned because the recruits don't get to pick and choose who their buddy is going to be.

The idea is to have one particular man to talk to—and complain to—during training. The battle buddy is also always expected to be aware of your whereabouts, and your mental and physical condition. You and he can provide encouragement to each other, keep one another out of trouble when off-duty, and have someone to rely upon. Later on, when in real combat, you can count on the fact that your battle buddy has your back and you've got his. It's an army-imposed "friendship." When a soldier goes through the nine-week Ranger course, he is assigned a Ranger Buddy. Same concept, and same purpose, just by a different name. The concept works and has served the soldiers of our army well for decades.

As a matter of fact, Jesus seemed to think it was a good idea, too. His disciples weren't exactly in a physical conflict—although most of them died torturous deaths under persecution later on. But Jesus knew all about spiritual warfare. And when he sent his followers out to share His message with the world, what did he do? He sent them in pairs, not one by one.

He also told those who followed Him—men and women alike—that when as few as two or three of them were praying together in His name, He would be in the midst of them, hearing their prayers and answering them. That Scripture is not meant to indicate God does not hear nor answer our individual prayers; rather it is an exhortation to unity and teamwork.

So maybe the idea of battle buddies came from a higher source than the Pentagon.

Stu Weber's book challenged me in several ways, but one idea really got my attention. Stu wrote, "As a Christian man, if there's a boy in your neighborhood without a father, you have the responsibility to mentor him."

I hadn't thought much about intentionally mentoring anyone, but the idea struck a chord with me. Because, in fact, I had noticed a young boy who lived near my townhouse in Alexandria, Virginia, and he seemed to be very much on his own. So, with Stu's challenge in mind, one day I struck up a conversation with him.

His name is Grant, and before long he was telling me all about his dad, how much he missed him and hoped to see him again soon. I began to spend more and more time with the boy. I took him fishing, and he tagged along with me on errands while we got better acquainted. It wasn't long before I figured it out. Although he spoke often about his dad, the man Grant had in mind wasn't much of a father at all. He left his family behind, and it was clear he was never coming back.

Gradually, I got to know the boy's sister Mimi, and by then I'd also met Grant's mother, Ashley, who was a heroic single mother, bringing up those two kids entirely on her own. I came to love them all. In fact, as it turned out, Ashley and I got married four years later in 1998. Her family has been my family ever since.

During my first year back at Fort Bragg, I was commanding all the U.S. Army's Green Berets. One day my chaplain said to me in passing, "We're bringing in a guy to speak to us. He used to be in the Special Forces in Vietnam and he's a pastor now, somewhere out west. His name is Stu Weber. Ever heard of him?"

I was stunned. "Stop right there!" I told him. "Just let me know when he's coming. I'll definitely be there."

When the day finally arrived, I was most certainly present. I couldn't wait to talk to this man, whose book had changed the course of my life.

"You don't know me, but my name is Jerry Boykin," I told him once we met. "Would you please come to my office?"

He said, "When?" And I said, "It doesn't matter—I'll cancel everything I've got. I just want to talk to you."

When Stu finally walked into my office, I said, "I owe you!" Then I told him the story. "I wouldn't have thought about reaching out to a neighborhood boy and I wouldn't be married to my wife, if it hadn't been for your book!"

And that wasn't the end of it. Not at all. In fact, it was the beginning of a rare and sacred friendship. Today, Stu Weber is one of my
battle buddies with a tremendous influence on my life. I am also
one of his battle buddies—more about that below. He lives on the
West Coast and I live in Virginia, but we manage to stay in close
contact because we've developed a deep and candid relationship. We
share things with each other, confide in each other, and encourage
each other. We give each other counsel. I covet his advice because
I've learned to depend on Stu. In fact, we have become hunting and
fishing buddies. I fly all the way across the country to elk hunt or
sturgeon fish with Stu just so we can spend quality one-on-one time
together. It is important to both of us to share our thoughts with
each other, including our fears and struggles.

But the most important thing is I know he won't compromise
the things I tell him. I also know he won't judge me; he's going to
understand what I'm saying and give me advice and counsel. And I'm
going to do the same for him.

We are not limited to a single battle buddy. In my case I have
two and have developed solid and intimate relationships with both.
Along with Stu Weber, I have another friend who has been by my
side through stormy seas even longer than Stu. His name is Yale King
and like Stu, he lives a good distance from me, in Colorado. We
have to communicate by phone and capitalize on every opportunity
to spend time together. Yale is amazing in that God often reveals
things to him regarding me, including issues I need to be aware of
and maybe concerned about. Also, Yale is often prompted to call me

or reach out to me when I am really struggling with a situation or a decision.

One of the times God used him was the day in 1993 after I was wounded in a mortar attack in Mogadishu. I was laying on my bunk unable to walk without crutches, feeling very alone and questioning God on so many issues. I finally prayed, "Lord, just give me something that will help me reach closure on all that has happened." Soon after I said that short prayer, one of my soldiers approached me with a piece of paper in his hand. "Colonel, I have a fax for you from Colorado." I took it from him and began to read it. It contained a Scripture from Isaiah 40:31 (NKJV), which says, "For they that wait upon the Lord shall renew their strength, they shall mount up on wings like eagles, they shall run and not grow weary, and they shall walk and not faint."

It was signed "Your Brother in Christ, Yale." God really used him at a critical time. And when I was going through a divorce he knew my heart was broken. So, he would fly to Washington to spend a weekend with me to comfort me during that troubled time. Our relationship is intimate, just as with Stu. God uses him and I try to allow God to use me in his life.

Do you have a Yale or a Stu in your life?

Believing in friendship and finding friends

How do you find your Stu Weber or Yale King? Maybe you are wondering whether you even need a battle buddy like that. Well, remember King David had Jonathan, with whom he made a covenant and whom he loved deeply. In spite of their best efforts to cast this as a homosexual relationship, the purveyors of this notion are dead wrong. Remember Joshua? He had a battle buddy in Caleb. In both of these cases, these men were like-minded and shared a deep faith. Men today need the same thing, a battle buddy with whom they can share their thoughts, a man they can trust.

First of all, that kind of friendship doesn't happen every day. In any case, most friendships, however deep or long-lasting, don't happen overnight. In fact, it isn't always easy for some men to develop friendships. Most observers agree it's easier for women than men.

At best, it takes time. In fact, in some ways, men aren't sure what a real and lasting male friendship should be like. Writer Drew Hunter says it well:

> Many factors combine to make friendship difficult for men. Personally, time for friends seems unrealistic in light of work or family responsibilities. Culturally, we don't have a shared understanding of what friendships among men should look like. We also find ourselves connecting more digitally than deeply. We've lost a vision for strong, warm, face-to-face, and side-by-side, male friendship.[18]

I think men need to appreciate their need for friendship and its value. Once you begin to understand that, you're on a quest. That's when you start asking God to bring into your life the kind of friends you need. Even then, it requires some effort to build each relationship. You may already have some good friends you respect a lot and a few you really admire.

But developing any genuine male friendship is a little like a relationship with a woman: it takes time, and you have to invest in it. Men have a lot of distractions. Men also have short attention spans. In a lot of cases, more than a few men don't realize they have to be deliberate in building deep and long-term relationships.

I think Stu and I were mature enough to know what we were trying to achieve when we finally met some twenty years ago. The same applies to Yale. We came to a point where we needed a battle buddy and we felt the Lord brought us together. We invested in each other and in the relationship and out of that came the friendship we have today. We all realize it is a rare gift.

Aside from having a battle buddy, you're going to have other friends. Whoever they are, or how close you feel to them, you have a general responsibility for being concerned about their well-being, just as they ought to be concerned about you.

What qualities do we look for in friends? What roles do we hope they'll play in our lives? What do we have to offer them? I think it's fair to say there are many different kinds of friends. Just as we bring certain qualities to our friendships, different kinds of men with very different personalities may offer unique contributions, broadening our scope, and helping direct our steps.

- Some men find a way to build up our confidence in ourselves and in God, believing in us and telling us, now and then, why they do.
- Some men are naturally positive encouragers and help us look on the bright side—even in dark times.
- Some men really enjoy our company and we enjoy theirs because our personalities are compatible. And we always manage to laugh together.
- Some men are strategic thinkers who help us remember to look at the big picture.
- Some men are faithful companions and make themselves available when we don't feel like going it alone.
- Some men are natural networkers and genuinely enjoy introducing one friend to another.
- Some men are motivators who inspire us to try something new or to keep innovating in what we're already doing.
- Some men are true believers, who help us remember by faith in Christ that all things are possible.

Most of us already have friends whose company we enjoy from time to time. They're bright or funny or share our interests in some way or other. If we've been through some life experiences together and have a shared history, we may even turn out to be friends for life.

Some of us enjoy hunting and fishing with the same friends, year in and year out. Others have hobbies or occupations or experiences in common with us. And some of us have Christian friends who pray for us and touch our lives by being devoted intercessors. Sometimes they know we need prayer, even before we do.

Give it some thought—what kind of man, specifically speaking, would be a good friend to you? Or to whom could you be a good friend?

I think you want a guy who is a good listener. He recognizes he has two ears and one mouth. He really knows how to listen because he is truly interested in what you have to say. He's not like one of those guys whose lips start quivering the minute you say something because he is so anxious to take over the conversation.

You also want a guy who's of a good principled character. Of course, that doesn't mean he's perfect, or that at some point he's not going to have a malfunction. But he's willing to admit his weaknesses and because he's aware of them, he's looks out for his kind of temptation.

The kind of friend you're looking for knows you're also vulnerable, so he's not surprised by your weaknesses. He's the kind of man who's on guard, keeping watch over his own heart. He's thoughtful and self-aware and he understands and admits to his vulnerabilities.

If you're a serious Christian, it's also going to be a man who is Scripturally literate—not necessarily an authority on the Bible, but he does have a deep enough understanding to address your problems and his own from a biblical perspective. He may not know the exact chapter and verse, but he can tell you the general context, and he'll offer it in response to your request for his advice. That advice will also come from his own experiences in the real world. You don't want someone who just quotes Scripture but never shows understanding of the challenges men face in our earthly homes.

We have all seen those sanctimonious churchmen who are always talking a big game. You've probably run across a few of them too. They've got all the language and all the right things memorized. You put a quarter in the slot and out comes a Bible verse.

That's not who you're looking for.

Over time, as you and your friend become better acquainted, each of you is becoming aware of the other's characteristics and heart. Eventually, as far as you're concerned, God will show you whether this is a person you can trust, or conversely, whether you shouldn't trust him too much—or at all.

Maybe he's a Christian but you aren't comfortable because he likes to talk too much. Big talkers have a greater tendency to compromise you than the strong, silent types who aren't so eager to transmit the latest insider gossip. You have to think about those characteristics.

There are also people who always seem to need something. They manage to tell you their troubles whenever they catch up with you, and maybe even hint around that you can somehow intervene. They may think you're a power player or a psychologist or even a Bank of America cash machine, so they're hoping you'll hand over something they crave. These hapless characters may imagine you'll become the kind of friend who's obligated by the Lord of Hosts to help solve their problems.

Sometimes we just have to say "No" and mean it.

Of course, all kinds of men can be your "occasional" friends, and you may enjoy hanging out with them from time to time. However, in most cases, if you're struggling, who's your best confidant? A smooth talker? A guy who never quite gets the facts right? Are you going to turn to that coworker who keeps checking his iPhone for updates while you're talking to him?

Probably not.

In any case, you can talk to God about your quest for trustworthy friendships. He didn't put us on this earth to be islands but to be relational and connected with other people. He also knows—so much better than we do—our desire for friends has to be tempered by the realization a lot of people aren't suitable for a close, sometimes brutally honest relationship. His Word reminds us, "Iron sharpens iron."

Are his bad decisions really my business?

Most of us have managed to hang on to a few good friends. They may not be battle buddies, but they've found a way to stay in our lives, and we're in theirs for the long haul. When that's the case, we have certain responsibilities to them. Sometimes we have the pleasure of applauding their accomplishments or sharing happy occasions with them. But, when necessary, we also owe it to them to be truth-tellers. And we have to hope they'll be equally straightforward with us.

There's a fine line between a man being a defender—as I talked about in the last chapter—and being an honest, truth-telling friend, even when it isn't easy.

How does that play out? Here's one example: maybe one of your friends has started drinking too much lately. After watching an NFL playoff game with friends, where alcohol is plentiful, you know he shouldn't drive home. You tell him but he laughs it off. Since you know it's no laughing matter, you may have to take his car keys. He probably won't like it at the time, but he'll most likely appreciate it later. He'll realize you may well have saved him from a DUI, running over somebody, wrapping his car around a tree, or worse.

These days, it seems a lot of men would say, "Yeah, but his drinking habits are none of my business. He's an adult." Well, yes, he's an adult who needs someone to intervene in his life—right then and there. Maybe your friendship with him is influential enough to keep him from doing something really stupid. Keep that in mind, because it's important.

As I pointed out in the last chapter, you may also have to do your best to talk him out of things like drug abuse, adultery, pornography, and so forth. Again, a lot of men would say, "I'm not getting involved. He's a big boy, he'll figure it out." But if you know he's going to hurt himself—not to mention his friends and family—it's your job as a friend to intervene.

For instance, what happens when you know a married friend of yours is doing something he shouldn't be doing, like seeing another woman on the side? What's your role? Sure, you can pray for him. But if you're a real friend, you certainly have a responsibility to try to help open his eyes.

You'll find yourself saying something like this: "You're not going to like what I'm about to tell you…" And you wrap it up as quickly as possible.

He may say, "Look, my wife and I haven't been intimate in a long time. And I'm not cut out for the life of a monk."

That's when I'd say, "So is she still your wife? Did you make a commitment to her, for better or worse? In sickness and in health? If you made that commitment, you're going to have to forgo dalliances. You can't do what you're doing without paying the price somewhere down the line. I'm telling you this as a friend. I've seen it happen before. Get counseling with your wife. It actually works for many." Many churches now have a counseling ministry.

Hard as it may be, I think you'll be glad in the long run. Because what you're doing is keeping your friend from destroying his family. Anyway, that's how you speak to a friend, man to man.

It's not just about women. Some men can become increasingly self-indulgent and you notice over time they're spending more and more money on personal pastimes. They always want the very best gear available to enhance their hobby. Fishing. Golf. Hunting. Photography. Collecting fossils. Whatever it is, once they've bought every gadget or artifact they can possibly find, they move on to the next diversion, and on it goes. Before long, your friend—or your friend's wife—is trying to figure out how to pay the bills by month's end.

Of course, you can't always stop somebody from making foolish mistakes and choices, but as a friend, you really do have a responsibility to try. You may be able to protect a very good friend from making a very bad life decision, and you've got to hope someday he'll find the courage to do the same for you.

You may hear your friend say, "I got a DUI...I made a bad mistake." I hope you'll bear in mind there's a big difference between a mistake and a choice. I remember hearing the governor of South Carolina claim he was hiking along the Appalachian Trail when he was actually in Argentina, shacked up in a hotel with his mistress. He got on TV and cried a few tears and said, "I've made a terrible mistake. I'm like the great King David."

I'm thinking, "No, you made a terrible *choice*. There was no mistake! You knew it was wrong when you did it. And, to make matters worse, you really shouldn't be comparing yourself to the great King David. Give me a break!"

These are the same men who say, "Well, you know what happened? Suddenly...I found myself in bed with her!" No, that's way too mystical for my taste. You consciously and deliberately made the choice to do what you did. You did it because you let your carnal nature prevail. Even though we are men of faith, we must contend with that nature and be vigilant in beating it down from time to time. Trust me; I know. You just have to do what Joseph did when Potiphar's wife put the big hit on him, trying to get him into her bed—*he ran*! Hey bro, you too can run from that—but you have to want to.

You see, a mistake is when you can't balance your checkbook correctly and the math doesn't add up. A bad choice is a calculated decision. And that's something people have to understand when they say, "Well, you know, everybody makes mistakes." Okay, fair enough. But not everybody *consciously opts* to make bad choices.

We also need to be encouragers to our friends. Some of them have hopes and dreams, yet although they've prayed and watched and waited, there's been no answer from above. I think most of us want instant gratification. We even want it in our walk with Christ. Sometimes we get quick and miraculous answers to our prayers. The more typical story is one of persistence and steadfastness; pray, watch, and wait.

Do you remember the story of Elijah? He was up on Mount Carmel waiting for God to send the rain He'd promised. Elijah told his servant, "Go look. Do you see any rain clouds?" His servant came back to him six times and said, "Nope." Elijah sent him out yet again. That time the servant came back and said, "Well, yeah. I did see a cloud the size of a man's fist...." After seven tries, the rain was finally on its way.

Jesus's disciple, James, retells that story and also provides some good advice for how Christian friends can help one another:

> Is anyone among you sick? Let them call the elders
> of the church to pray over them and anoint them
> with oil in the name of the Lord. And the prayer
> offered in faith will make the sick person well; the
> Lord will raise them up. If they have sinned, they
> will be forgiven. Therefore, confess your sins to each

other and pray for each other so that you may be healed. The prayer of a righteous person is powerful and effective. Elijah was a human being, even as we are. He prayed earnestly that it would not rain, and it did not rain on the land for three and a half years. Again, he prayed, and the heavens gave rain, and the earth produced its crops.

—James 5:14-18 (NIV)

Sometimes our circumstances really do change almost as soon as we pray; answers seem to materialize within hours or even minutes when the need is pressing. But more often than not, it's a matter of getting back on our knees over and over again, and persistently asking the Lord for what we need. Before it's over, we're going to have to repeat what Christ cried out in the Garden of Gethsemane, "Not my will, but thine, be done" (Luke 22:42 [KJV]).

God never promised us there wouldn't be casualties in the battle between His kingdom and the kingdoms of this world. He did promise us ultimate victory, but we need to grasp the necessity for persistence, and to accept the possibility we may suffer serious wounds along the way.

After a while, most of us can often look back and say, "Thank you God! I'm so very grateful you didn't answer that prayer the way I wanted you to!" But at the time we were upset with Him because, in our disappointment, He seemed to have coldly turned His back on us.

To make matters worse, the world is moving very quickly nowadays. We're rushing around with a twenty-four-hour TV news cycle playing in the background, living on the edge of our seats in an instant-gratification society, and we want everything on the first try. If we have to wait for it, we feel like we've been abandoned by God. Of course, we haven't, but it sure feels like it.

Believe me—I've been there.

"If there's no God, there's no hope."

In Mogadishu, Somalia, fifteen of my men were killed in an eighteen-hour firefight represented in the movie *Black Hawk Down*. Needless to say, I prayed for a different and far better outcome. When I saw the mangled bodies of those men returning to our base, it broke me spiritually. That night, after we recovered all but two of our dead and saw our wounded evacuated, I sat down on my bunk to have a serious discussion with God. My anger toward Him was real and powerful. "God, where were you? Didn't you care?" I asked as my tears began to flow.

"How could you let this happen?" My anger grew as the feeling God let me down intensified.

"Where were you, God?"

A rogue thought came into my mind immediately, "There is no God. If there was a God, this wouldn't have happened."

We all have a tendency to think that way. We don't believe our prayers got past the ceiling. We imagine God has better things to do. Most of the time we need to stop fretting and complaining and listen for the Lord's voice. Of course, eventually He'll give us guidance and direction. But His wisdom may not be the first thing that comes into our minds.

We search our souls. "Am I really doing what you've called me to do or are you ignoring me because I'm somehow outside of your will?"

That's a hard thing to resolve because a man wants to do what a man wants to do. I know I do. I think my struggle in Mogadishu had a lot to do with His will versus my will. Sometimes God doesn't give us success or victory as we want because he has something else in mind for us.

And sometimes, for reasons we may never understand, there's just no happy ending.

That night, when I angrily said, "There's no God!" I immediately heard a still small voice, "If there's no God, there's no hope."

If there's no God, there's no hope. I knew His Spirit was speaking to me.

I began to weep and to repent. "I'm sorry…I'm sorry I denied you." I felt like Peter. He walked with Jesus for three and a half years, watching Him perform incredible miracles, and then, after sitting for ninety minutes by a fire with a hostile crowd around him, he somehow managed to deny his Lord three times. He even cursed.

But then, in the Book of Acts, we read the report of how Peter went on to preach a sermon that brought 3,000 people into Jesus's kingdom—the spiritual kingdom He promised to everyone who would follow Him. What happened? Well, Peter repented. And later, after His resurrection, Jesus graciously restored Peter into His service. Yet even that didn't happen overnight.

I'm like most guys who want to see my prayers answered right now, to see success right away. Unfortunately, it doesn't work like that. We have to be persistent. He's told us not to give up.

We should never surrender, except to Him.

I can assure you once you surrender to Him, you'll have the strength to carry on, even when you don't see a positive outcome. Of course, we get frustrated and start complaining, "I'm wasting my time." But it won't go on like that forever. Eventually God's going to confront our enemy, Satan, and tell him, "Okay, back off. That's enough!"

In Mogadishu on that terrible night, after crying out, "There's no God!" I heard that voice, of the Lord, saying, "If there's no God, there's no hope." I found myself sobbing, weeping so powerfully I was literally shaking all over.

I picked up my Bible and I said, "I'm sorry, but I don't understand. Give me something in Your Word."

I opened the book without looking for a specific passage; I just opened it randomly. To Proverbs 3:5-6 (KJV). "Trust in the Lord with all thine heart; and lean not unto thine own understanding. In all thy ways acknowledge him, and he shall direct thy paths." That quickly, He gave me the answer. I understood Him to say, "What happened here is within my will."

We simply must understand we do not have the mind of God and therefore there are things we will never understand. All we can do is remind ourselves God is sovereign. God doesn't bring bad things upon us. I'm not one who subscribes to the idea "Well, God brought that down on you to teach you a lesson." Get over it. He doesn't deal in evil. That's not only important for us to understand at the time; it's also important for us to remember those intensely challenging experiences so we can retell them later on, in order to help and encourage others.

In 2011, I stood over my forty-nine-year-old sister and watched her pass into eternity from breast cancer. A finer Christian woman would be hard to find. With just the two of us in the room, I questioned God, "Why are you taking her, Lord? She has done so much for so many and has been so faithful to you. It's just not right."

And then I felt in my spirit God was speaking to me in the still small voice the Bible talks about. I believe God was saying, "You are seeing this from your own perspective; I am bringing her home to her just reward. Do you really want her to stay here?" Once again, I questioned God's wisdom. Right then I felt so small in His presence.

The case for mentoring

> *When they saw him, they worshiped him; but some doubted. Then Jesus came to them and said, "All authority in heaven and on earth has been given to me. Therefore go and make disciples of all nations, baptizing*

them in the name of the Father and of the Son and of the Holy Spirit."

—*Matthew 28:17-19 (NIV)*

The Great Commission is something we all need to understand because it is the directive Jesus left his disciples before he ascended to be with the Father. In my view, it is a call to mentor others. How do you make disciples? You have to mentor them. Start with showing them the way to salvation and then help them understand how to make Christ the Lord of their lives:

If you declare with your mouth, "Jesus is Lord," and believe in your heart that God raised him from the dead, you will be saved

—Romans 10:9 (NIV)

Joshua is my favorite biblical character. Just think about the awesome responsibility thrust on him when Moses informed him that he, Joshua, would lead the Israelites across the Jordan to conquer the Promised Land.

For forty years Joshua walked in the footsteps of the great leader, Moses, expecting Moses to lead the conquest of Canaan. Suddenly Moses was telling Joshua the task was now his because God was calling Moses home. I just cannot fathom what must have gone through Joshua's mind, but the reality is he was ready for the mission. The reason is he was mentored by that great man of faith, Moses.

In fact, Joshua would even follow Moses into the Tent of Meeting (Exodus 23:7). This was where Moses went to meet with God before the first tabernacle was built. In Exodus 33:11, we read Joshua would remain in the tent after Moses left. What was Joshua doing? He was emulating his mentor. Those forty years of being in the shadow of Moses prepared him for the greatest task of his life: a task bringing an end to the wandering of the Jewish people and a new beginning in the Covenant Land.

That story serves as a biblical example of godly mentoring and brings with it the expectation that Christian men can and should be mentors to those who are new to the faith or are fatherless. Or to those who just need the mentoring of someone who can help them with their struggles in life. Are you mentoring anyone? You should be, or you should at least be looking for that opportunity.

And please don't think because you've had setbacks or failures you can't be a mentor. That line of reasoning is a trick of the enemy. All men have had failures of one kind or another. I certainly have. But 1 John 1:9 (NKJV) tells us, "If we confess our sins, he is faithful and just to forgive us our sins, and to cleanse us of all unrighteousness."

I hope you'll pray for God to send you someone to mentor or even for someone to mentor you.

Mentoring is another way of being a friend, but much more than a friend. Mentoring is a unique opportunity for us to share our own experiences—the good ones and the bad ones—in order to provide counsel, to offer encouragement, and to be a blessing to another man or young boy. I think it's something many men overlook.

It was a lesson I first learned from my battle buddy Stu Weber, whose book inspired me to get acquainted with that young neighborhood boy many years ago—Grant—and to become a mentor to him. Years later, it happened again.

Not long after I retired, I was speaking at a men's conference in Richmond, Virginia, focusing my teaching about men becoming "Kingdom Warriors." At the end of that session, a man came up to me and said, "My name is Steve, and I'm with the Virginia State Police. I don't know why, but I feel like the Lord just told me to come up here and ask if you'd be willing to mentor me."

I'd never seen the man before. I hadn't recently thought much about mentoring, but I answered right away, "Yeah, sure. I will."

And so began my mentoring relationship with Steve. I didn't see him often, but we kept in touch by phone and email. He turned out to be one of the chaplains who ministered to the state police. And he was a man's man. He'd been a linebacker at Wake Forest and probably would have had a professional career had he not made one questionable decision between his junior and senior years.

At that time, he was working as a bouncer at a bar. During some sort of scuffle, in the heat of battle he smacked a troublemaker. Unfortunately, the big shot he smacked turned out to be president of Wake Forest Booster Club. In case you don't know, the Booster Club pays the head football coach's salary. That one quick incident ruined Steve's chance to play professional football. Instead, he spent most of his year with a lackluster performance because he missed spring practice due to suspension. That was the end of his football career.

By the time I met Steve, he was still very much a man's man. He was a big, fit guy. While serving as a state policeman, he came to Christ, and became a faithful Christian, although, like all of us, he was still learning. He volunteered to serve as a chaplain for the police, which meant he would officiate at funerals and fulfill a number of other responsibilities and obligations on a volunteer basis.

Before long, a new state police superintendent took charge. For some reason, he put out a decree saying something like "You chaplains can no longer pray in the name of Jesus."

I first heard about that disturbing announcement on the news. Then a short time later while I was driving, I got to thinking about Steve. I knew he had to be struggling with that new edict. Right then, at that moment, I had the impulse to check on him. I punched his number into my car phone.

When he answered, I said, "Steve, what are you doing?"

"So…" he began, "Funny you should ask. I'm just getting ready to hit 'send' on an email to the superintendent. I'm gonna' tell him that I'm not going to be a chaplain anymore."

That would have stopped me in my tracks had I not been speeding in the fast lane.

"Steve, don't do that!" I told him. "Instead, go in and see the superintendent personally. That's the manly thing to do. Tell him to his face if you can't pray according to your faith, you respectfully resign. But don't burn any bridges other than by resigning."

Because of the mentoring relationship we shared, I believe the Lord laid Steve on my heart at the very moment he was about to press the "send" button. Instead, Steve erased the email, made an appointment, and soon went in to explain his situation to his new boss.

Had Steve put his situation in writing and sent it off in an email, it would have proliferated—there's no such thing as an email between only two people, especially if there's a controversy involved. In fact, even so, Steve's refusal to continue as a chaplain became a big story in the state of Virginia. The media managed to find a way to position Steve as the ringleader of a revolt against the new state police superintendent. Unsurprisingly, that's the way some journalists chose to spin it.

As it turned out, some of the other chaplains followed suit. But, again, had Steve sent that initial email, it would have looked like there was some kind of conspiracy, with similar emails stirring up other chaplains with the intention of launching a protest. So, to stop the story's momentum right then and there, I encouraged him to have another one-on-one conversation with the superintendent and leave it at that.

Later on, there was a race to elect a new governor of Virginia, and Bob McDonnell was one of the contenders. In fact, he eventually won. But while he was running for office, he recognized Steve at a campaign rally. He walked over to him and said, "I know what you did about the state police chaplaincy and I respect you for that. And I'm looking forward to your becoming the next state police superintendent if I become governor."

Steve never became the state police superintendent. He has since retired from the police force and served at Liberty University as the

Director of Public Safety. But I'll always remember how God brought us together and I became a mentor to him. In the ten years we've had a mentoring relationship, our friendship has become close and meaningful. The Holy Spirit will often prompt me to call this man and it always turns out to be at a moment when he is in a battle of some kind. He's also there when I need him, with wise counsel. We always discuss the situation and then we pray.

Thankfully, he is still doing well. Yet he still experiences warfare frequently because he is such a strong warrior in the kingdom and he is making such a difference.

What made Steve want me to be his mentor? First of all, he had the strong impression God was specifically leading him to ask me if I'd be willing take on that role. Also, his career in law enforcement probably caused him to look for someone who could understand his responsibilities and his role, which occasionally required violence and physical confrontation. My military background, and perhaps something he'd heard me say, led him to want my guidance in his life. And I had the strong impression it would be good for us both if I could provide it.

Mentoring—a matter of life and death

Being a mentor isn't just about one grown man giving another grown man advice about his career, love life, or important decisions. Not long ago the need for a mentor in a young man's life felt like an emergency to me. I could hardly believe what I was hearing when a troubled boy poured out his heart.

I was speaking in Chicago at a men's conference, where I learned a generous donor had made it possible for about thirty young black men, from around thirteen to sixteen years old, to attend. They were all from the south side of Chicago—they came to us out of the proverbial "hood." Since the conference's leaders wanted to make sure those young men would get the kind of guidance they needed, they asked me if I'd take the time to talk to them directly. We took them out of the larger audience into a separate room.

I talked to those guys for about ninety minutes and then I asked them if there was anything they wanted me to talk about. As I listened to their questions, I got a pretty good sense of what their lives were like. As the others shared their experiences, one young boy didn't say a word. Something about him caught my attention. At the end of the session, as he started to walk out of the room I said, "Son, come over here. I need to tell you something."

He politely walked over to me, but still didn't say anything. I went ahead and told him what was on my mind anyway.

"You're not going to understand what I'm about to say to you," I began, "but I believe you have a calling on your life. I just feel it. I have a sense the Holy Spirit is showing me..." I paused for a moment, then I went on to say, "that you really need to seek God and search for what God wants to do with you. He has an anointing on you."

He looked a little puzzled, but just walked away, again without a word.

A little while later, while I was signing books, he came up to my book table. He quietly asked if he could talk to me privately.

I led him into a side room, where we sat down. He said, "Sir, my name is D'Andrea. I don't know who my dad is. I only see my mother four times a year—she's in prison. I live with my grandmother. And I'm thinking about committing suicide."

Well, that got my attention. I said, "D'Andrea, how old are you?"

He said, "I'll be thirteen next week."

I looked into his eyes in amazement. "How could life be so bad for you that you'd want to commit suicide?"

He said, "Well, there's gangs in my neighborhood. And every gang wants me to join them. If I say yes to one gang, the other one's gonna' beat me up—and if I say no to the first gang, *they'll* beat me up. So, every gang beats me up and I don't feel like I can take it anymore. I just don't want to live."

We sat in silence for a few moments. "Okay, I'm going to see what I can do for you, D'Andrea," I told him. "But for now, let's go back into the conference."

We walked back into the sanctuary together and in a few minutes the next part of our program began, during which I spoke briefly. Then I called some of our men forward and asked them to offer a father's blessing to those boys or men who never before received it. The father's blessing is another story, which I'll describe in the next chapter.

As the men were making their way to the front of the room. I brought D'Andrea up there and I laid my hands on him and gave him a father's blessing myself, along with a strong affirmation. For obvious reasons, it was pretty emotional for him and for me.

As I prayed over him I said, "You're a man—you're a man with whom God is greatly pleased. Now may you find His will in your life. May you search for Him and find Him. The Bible says, 'You will find me when you seek with all your heart.'"

When I got through, with D'Andrea standing next to me, I challenged that gathering of men. "I need somebody to mentor this young man."

Nobody raised his hand. I knew exactly why. Nobody wanted to go into D'Andrea's neighborhood. So, I said it again, "The Lord is calling someone here to mentor this young man."

Finally, a white man, who was there with his son, raised his hand. He walked up to the front and said, "Yes. I'll mentor him."

I got the two of them linked up and made arrangements for this good man to go into D'Andrea's neighborhood and start spending time with him. My whole purpose in doing that was to put a male in a position of authority who could be a role model for the young man. It had to be someone who would go to D'Andrea's home, gain the trust of his grandmother, spend quality time with him, and help him establish the values godly men are supposed to have.

Above all else, D'Andrea needed to trust the Lord and learn to rely on Him.

Let them endure hardship

A couple of years ago I was sitting around a fire in Alaska with two of my sons, my brother, and some friends, after a great day of fishing for salmon on the Kenai River. At some point the conversation shifted to the U.S. Army Ranger School, one of the toughest and most demanding courses in the army.

My son completed the course in 1997, twenty-five years after I graduated from the same course. Aaron was in a particularly bad class that started with over 220 students and only graduated about 48. The weather was miserable during their training, with heavy snow in the mountain phase and cold rain and winds in the other phases. Most of those who failed simply quit. They were not mentally prepared for what they encountered.

I was complementing Aaron for completing the course. He looked at me and asked, "Dad, do you know why I made it?"

"Well, yeah. You're a tough guy."

He smiled and began to explain what he was leading up to. "You remember all those mornings you got me out of bed a 5 a.m., took me out into the woods, and put me in a tree stand where I sat all day hoping a deer would come by? And the whole time I was shivering. Or how about when you took me to a duck blind where my feet would nearly freeze? And there were those hikes of several days on the Appalachian Trail when you made Randy and me carry what seemed like incredibly heavy rucksacks?"

I acknowledged I remembered with a nod. I think I may have mumbled, "Sorry, son."

Then he gave me the punch line. "Dad, I made it through Ranger School because I knew I could! I endured hardship before. Most of these guys had never been challenged and they were just not mentally tough enough to keep going when things got miserable."

The point is we need to let those we care about endure enough hardship so they'll learn to cope with difficulties. Sometimes it means letting them suffer the consequences of their own bad choices. It could be letting them spend a night in jail when they are charged with a DUI or for smoking marijuana or for childish vandalism.

Do not try to spare them the painful consequences of doing things they know are wrong! In the end it may well be something they reflect on in the future—something that helps them choose the right path or to refuse to quit when situations arise that test their courage and determination.

Keeping man-to-man friendships alive

Are you willing to choose to be a mentor and to see a challenging commitment through, no matter how stressful it may become? Are you going to pick up the phone and keep in touch with a couple of old friends, just for the sake of enjoying the occasional company of like-minded guys? And once you are finally able to locate your battle buddy—the one who'll walk beside you through thick and thin—will you hang in there, even when your life changes and you're either busy and distracted or depressed and feeling like you've got nothing to say?

I've come to believe our friendships with men should be high on our list of thanksgiving prayers. Male friends are among our greatest gifts from God. They don't come easy. And, like so many other life commitments, those relationships require more than superficial conversations, raucous laughter, or even the occasional awkwardness of sharing deeply personal circumstances. Male relationships also require endurance and a serious commitment to longevity.

Sometimes we call it "stick-to-it-ness." But when it comes to our man-to-man friendships, just the act of keeping in touch, and making sure our connections are strong and healthy, can be a challenge—perhaps more so than in our other relationships. Why? Because men find it so easy to get distracted or are constantly dealing with other obligations or even become temporarily disinterested.

We have to make a conscious, decisive effort to keep our commitments to our friends alive—just as we need to nurture our other personal obligations—no matter what.

As usual, my real-life battle buddy Stu Weber says it best. Here's what he wrote in *Tender Warrior:*

> Staying power. The bottom line? Stay with it, man.
> Stick by your commitments. Stand by your promises.
> Never, never let go, no matter what. When marriage
> isn't fun...stay in it. When parenting is over your
> head...stay at it. When work is crushing your

spirit…don't let it beat you. When the local church is overwhelmed with pettiness…stay by it. When your children let you down…pick them up. When your wife goes through a six-month mood swing…live with it. When it's fourth and fourteen with no time on the clock…throw another pass.

MAN AS A BATTLE BUDDY—
A WORD FOR WOMEN

There are always exceptions, but it's often said men are less likely than women to have close friends—guys with whom they can speak frankly, and openly, about anything, and everything. They may have pals at work they banter with or a team that participates in a sport or outdoor activity. Their brothers or uncles or cousins may have family traditions that bring them together from time to time.

But many men lack a male confidant. Instead they may keep their worries or problems to themselves. Your boyfriend or husband may think of you as his best friend—which is a wonderful compliment. However, as the saying goes, "Iron sharpens iron," and men need a male perspective from time to time, or they may need to talk about something they'd feel more comfortable talking about with another man.

Sometimes girlfriends and wives feel left out or uncomfortable when they see close male friendships developing between their "significant others" and other men. There may even be feelings of jealousy, or rivalry, and a fear of lost "togetherness." We need to remember every man will be enlarged and blessed by a male confidant, with whom he shares common ground and, best of all, a spiritual bond.

General Boykin writes about a battle buddy, and in fact many men who have served in the military deeply cherish the friendships of those with whom they've shared some powerful and even life-threatening experiences. Those men will be lifelong buddies, no matter what.

If you have a close female friend, you know from experience how she enriches your life. Does your husband have a male confidant? Are your sons developing close male friendships? If not, they may be missing out on one of life's most vital and essential gifts. I hope you'll look for ways to encourage those friendships and be grateful when they flourish.

Man as a Battle Buddy—
Discussion Questions

1. This chapter focuses on men relating to other men. What is meant by "battle buddy"? Can you remember some biblical support for the concept?

2. Stu Weber advises, "As a Christian man, if there's a boy in your neighborhood without a father, you have the responsibility to mentor him." Is there someone in your life you should be mentoring?

3. Men today need a battle buddy with whom they can share their thoughts and who they can trust. What were some famous biblical examples of battle buddies? Are there some guys you would consider battle buddies in your orbit of relationships?

4. Do you have a battle buddy? If not, is there someone in your life who could fill that void? What kind of man would be a good friend to you? Or to whom could you be a good friend? Considering the characteristics of a battle buddy discussed in this chapter, which three do you value most when it comes to male friendship?

5. Thinking of your battle buddy, do you hold each other accountable, or do you look the other way when bad decisions are made? How can you hold each other and even your other friends and family members accountable?

6. In addition to holding each other accountable, we need to be encouragers to our friends. What are some specific ways you can encourage those around you?

7. One of the main ways we can encourage other men is through prayer. When you say you will pray for another man in need, do you do it? Try this: pray with the guy on the spot. It will mean a lot more for him to hear you pray at that moment than it will to hear you promise to pray and walk away.

8. Have you ever doubted or denied the Lord? Be honest; we all have, and that's the point. There are men who go through those same dark valleys who need a battle buddy to come alongside with understanding, encouragement, perspective, and prayer. Do you know a guy who is hurting and needs a battle buddy?

9. Is there a younger man in your orbit of relationships who is asking to be mentored by you? He may not straight out ask, but based on the contact and communication, it is becoming clear. Or is there someone who evidently needs a mentor you might approach for the purpose of suggesting it, and if amenable, getting started?

10. It is important to let those you mentor endure hardship in a controlled fashion, in order to prepare them for what life may throw at them. What are some healthy examples of this concept?

CHAPTER FIVE

MAN AS A CHAPLAIN

*Let vice and immorality of every kind be discouraged
as much as possible in your brigade; and, as a chaplain
is allowed to each regiment, see that the men regularly
attend during worship. Gaming of every kind is expressly
forbidden, as being the foundation of evil, and the cause
of many a brave and gallant officer's and soldier's ruin.*

—*George Washington*[19]

*The righteous man walks in his integrity; his children
are blessed after him.*

—*Proverbs 20:7 (NKJV)*

I t was 1978. After months of uncertainty and prayer and after weeks of a grueling, almost indescribably difficult selection process, I was very close to the conclusion of the endurance trial of a lifetime. I was still standing. All that remained was my final interview with the U.S. Army officers who were tasked with finally determining which fighters would comprise a new and controversial U.S. commando unit.

It would be called Delta Force.

I was highly successful at the physical aspects of the selection—which concluded with a brutal forty-mile march. But after an interview with a psychologist, my enthusiasm was chilled by his words. Based on his analysis, he told me, "You will not fit in here. You rely too much on your faith and not enough on yourself." My heart sank at his final remarks.

"I'm going to recommend against your being a part of this organization."

Still, I knew it wasn't over 'til it was over. Another interview awaited, and that time I was face to face with a group of commissioned and non-commissioned officers, including the founder of the new unit. Notoriously brusque and cantankerous, he was a legend: Colonel Charlie Beckwith.

I sat facing the panel of men who bombarded me with questions. It almost seemed hostile, an effort to intimidate me. As each of the questioners asked me about my thoughts on issues, I realized there were no right and wrong answers to most of the questions. Suddenly, Colonel Beckwith stopped the questioning rather abruptly. Looking me square in the eye, Beckwith asked me point blank, "Captain Boykin, you're a religious man, aren't you?"

"Here it comes," I thought. "The bottom line." Right about then, I had some unholy thoughts about the psychologist.

"Yes, sir, I guess I am," I told him. Not that I was unsure. I just didn't like the way he'd framed the question. Lots of people are religious, but they have no faith in God.

"Is that the way you were raised?" Beckwith continued.

"Well, Colonel, I'll tell you, my mother is a saint. And yes, that's the way she raised me."

For reasons I couldn't guess, Beckwith paused for a long moment. Then he said, rather quietly. "Yeah, so was mine."

With that, he stood. "Captain Boykin, we'd be glad to have you," he said. When he walked over and shook my hand, joy and relief washed over me. I stood and shook the hands of the others. Their words were music to my ears; "Welcome to Delta!"

Out of a hundred and eighteen candidates, just nineteen of us made the cut.

We spent the next months in intense training, preparing ourselves for every kind of crisis. It wasn't long before the worst-case scenario rolled around. Immediately we were giving our full attention to preparations for Delta's first operation. It was as risky and difficult as anything we could have envisioned.

In February 1979, the government of Iran was overthrown by a radical Shi'ite Imam—Ruhollah Khomeini—who would be known thereafter as Iran's Supreme Leader. His Islamic Revolution was a bloodbath. In the process, on November 4, 1979, a throng of Khomeini's fiery youthful followers invaded the U.S. Embassy, kidnapping fifty-three Americans and holding them hostage.

Delta's first assignment was to rescue them. I've written elsewhere about the challenges we faced and the disappointments we endured. But one unexpected incident remains in my memory.

We were in Egypt, preparing to deploy into the Iranian desert refueling area; from there our complex rescue plan would take us to Teheran, and the American Embassy, after a few hours of hiding in the mountains outside of the city. Our staging base in Egypt was an old Russian MiG airfield. I was going through final checks on my gear when Charlie Beckwith walked up to me. "Jerry," he said, "I'm going to get all these men together tomorrow morning before we launch and I want you to say a prayer before we go."

I was astonished. Not since he and I talked about our mothers had Charlie expressed any interest at all in religion in general or my faith in particular, in fact most of the time I still wondered where I stood with him. He startled me with a side of him I never dreamed existed—Charlie conceded he and his men would do well this time to enlist the help of a higher authority.

"Okay, Colonel," I told him. "I'll be ready."

Early the next morning, he gathered Delta in the hangar in a loose formation and climbed up on a makeshift wooden platform. I stood off to Charlie's left. After he said some encouraging words to the men, he concluded, "We're ready for this mission. I have confidence in every one of you that you'll do your job and do it well."

Then he said, "I'm going to ask Jerry to come up here and say a prayer before we launch."

Before I could begin speaking, General James Vaught stepped forward. "I want to quote some Scripture," the general said. "In the book of Isaiah, the Bible says, 'And I heard the voice of the Lord saying, "Whom shall I send, and who will go for us?" And Isaiah said, "Here am I! Send me!" He continued, "Men, your country's counting on you. You've stepped forward and said, 'Here am I, send me.' God bless you!"

Vaught's words, which were from one of my favorite passages of the Bible, were a special blessing to me. For the second time in less than twenty-four hours, I was surprised to find faith at work. I knew there were other men of faith in Delta, but no one really talked about it. We didn't have an active Bible study and we didn't have a chaplain. But now, faced with a mission in which obstacles and danger hovered over every phase, even the senior officers among us swept our culture of absolute self-reliance aside and acknowledged God.

I asked the men to bow their heads and pray with me. "Almighty God, we've placed ourselves in your hands. And we ask you to lead us and guide us so that we might liberate our fellow Americans. We ask for your hand of mercy to be upon us. We ask for wisdom and courage. We ask you to keep us safe, and to keep safe the people we're going after. Bring us all home to our families. And I pray this in Christ's name, Amen."

After a rousing rendition of "God Bless America," a loud shout went up. Each man walked back to his cot, grabbed his gear, crossed the tarmac and marched into the back of the C-141.

* * *

That first Delta operation makes for a long and complicated story. Books have been written about it. Documentaries have focused on it. But as I reflect on those hours and days of preparation, it's clear to me that whatever the circumstances, God had a way of getting the attention of His warriors, reminding us He was holding our lives in His hands.

We can also see He found a way to appoint "chaplains" when He needed them, thrusting some of us forward to provide spiritual guidance and encouragement when it was most important. On that memorable occasion, I was grateful He chose to use me, but I felt totally inadequate at the time. It is just a reminder of how God does not necessarily choose the equipped; He equips the chosen. He also moved others to speak from His Word and to lift our spirits as we sang one of our country's most cherished prayers, "God Bless America."

The need for men who pray, who speak the Word and uplift those around them doesn't just apply to official military operations. The truth is everyday life in today's world is rife with conflict. I think it's safe to say our country and our Christian communities are in a battle for our spiritual lives, for the souls of our children and for the future of America. As Christian men, we serve as spiritual warriors in one way or another, no matter where we go or what our responsibilities may be. We'll take a closer look at the necessary preparations for spiritual warfare in the following chapter.

Meanwhile, our days may not be planned out like military operations. In fact, sometimes our most spiritually dangerous and intense conflicts take us by surprise. But as men of God, we need to be prepared to serve as spiritual leaders to those around us—whether we call ourselves chaplains, priests or pastors, spiritual counselors, or simply faithful and godly husbands and parents.

The family chaplain

Let's start with the family. Whether you're hoping to be a husband and father someday, you're already in that role, or you're older and finding joy in your grandchildren, I believe there is a specific spiritual call on fathers, grandfathers, and sons to serve as chaplains to their families. That's a God-ordained position for a man, and we have to remember it's a key biblical fact—the man of the house is intended to serve as the *Chaplain*—the spiritual head of the family. That doesn't mean the man makes all the decisions; nor does it mean he shouldn't share the responsibilities of the home with his wife. In fact, responsibility cuts both ways—she shares in his leadership role, particularly in the delegated management of the home, and he shares in her established role of nurturing the family including, among many other things, helping with children.

So how does the head of the house serve as his family's chaplain? First of all, every man needs to be a man of prayer and start with praying for and with his wife. In fact, he should be continually praying and interceding for each member of his family. He should pray first for their salvation if they don't know Christ as their Savior—that should be a priority. But there are many other things to pray for in daily life, and it falls on the man of the house to inquire and ask how he can be praying for each one in his home as the spiritual leader. Don't just say you will pray for them. They need to hear you do it.

By the way, that's not to say the mother shouldn't be praying for the family, too. In fact, Christian women tend to spend a lot more time in prayer than men, anyway. But the man needs to make it his passion to intercede for the eternal souls of his children and of his wife, too, if she is not yet in a relationship with Christ.

Dad also sets the spiritual climate within the home when the family is together. For example, that can come down to a fairly common question: are we going to have dinner around the table, in a setting where the father's going to pray a blessing over that meal? Or maybe everybody's just going to grab a TV tray, sit in front of the tube, and say, "Oh yeah, Lord—by the way—thanks for the food!"

I think a spiritual climate is developed in a home when the father sits down with his wife and children gathered around the table, everybody joins hands, and the father says the blessing over the food. That blessing can be a catalyst for further spiritual discussion, perhaps reading from the Bible or a good devotional book. Cultivating that spiritual climate will most likely be carried on to the next generation, once it's established what we, as a family, do.

But being a spiritual leader in the home isn't just about blessing food or leading a family devotion. As the family chaplain, Dad also needs to be willing to make some personal sacrifices. For example, in order to send a child to the best Christian summer program or private school, the father might have to sacrifice that new pickup truck he has had his eye on. I am not advocating that all children should go to Christian or charter schools, although I think that most of the public schools in America are failing our children. If he wants to be able to pay that tuition, he may have to look for a part-time job. It really comes down to his life's priorities, particularly when it comes to the spiritual formation of his children.

And it's very clear that this man—husband and head of the house—will need to make sacrifices for his wife. We learn about this in Ephesians 5:25 (NIV), "Husbands, love your wives as Christ loved the Church." How much did Christ love the Church? Enough to give his life for her. What does that mean? If you're prepared to give your life for your wife, there are more than a few good starting points. First of all, are you respecting her and showering her with love, attempting to meet her felt needs and teaching your children to do the same? Are you asking God to strengthen her, and nurture her, and help her continue to grow into the virtuous woman and mother who makes you and your children grateful and proud?

The family chaplain should be conscious that his right standing with God comes from his salvation through faith in Jesus Christ

(Romans 5:1). So we should all be praying that every day we'll be able to live a holier and more spiritual life because we know we're setting an honorable standard for the family. As the family chaplain sets the example, the wife and children should see a reflection of Christ in him. In the meantime, when we have those inevitable failures, as we all do, we confess it to God and get back in the game (1 John 1:9).

By the way, the man of the house is *not* a god or a deity. There are some elements within the broader Christian community that are way off the mark about this and they've become inappropriately patriarchal. These groups seem to think Dad is some godlike creature to be served and Mom is his servant to obey his every whim. Obviously, that's not what I'm talking about. That theology is unbiblical and unchristian. It bears repeating that the man needs to love his wife sacrificially, the way Christ loved his Church. He needs to demonstrate that in front of the children. He'll know he's got it right when his daughter says, "I want to marry a guy just like my dad." There's no greater honor.

The family chaplain—aka Dad—is also meant to provide vision for his family because in many ways he's serving as a prophet. I'm not talking about a fortune teller or some kind of weird psychic. I'm talking about a man who chooses to walk in close communion with God, asking Him to reveal His vision for the family. Don't even begin to think God has never given you a vision for your future or for the future of your family. If you have asked for that in your prayers, He has answered that prayer. Maybe you are not listening or maybe you don't like the answer he gave, but God loves the family so much He will not leave unanswered a prayer regarding the family's future.

If you're not sure, go back and try again. Pray for vision and then listen for the answer. It may come through a Scripture you have read a dozen times before and suddenly He reveals it. It may come through circumstances, through the doors God opens or the doors He shuts. Sometimes the answer will come through a godly person God sends your way. It may come through a dream God gives you. It frequently comes through the "still small voice" as Elijah discovered (1 Kings 19:12 [KJV]). But God is faithful to answer prayer and you need to expect an answer and then look for it.

Once God has revealed it to you, pray it over, think it through, then write it down. The next step for the family chaplain is to share it with his family and help his wife, sons, and daughters catch that God-given vision and make it their own. This means putting in place direction for the family, whether it's a purely commercial enterprise, a new business opportunity, or a spiritual adventure. Whatever it is, the man's got to be able to set that vision in a way the family can understand it and gladly buy into it.

Joshua serves as the perfect example of a patriarch casting a vision for the family when he calls the leaders of the Jewish tribes together right before his death and preaches his own epitaph. Joshua 24:15 (KJV) describes how this great leader instructed the tribal leadership who were assembled there in Shechem to choose which gods they would serve in the future. Speaking for his own family, he then revealed a clear vision when he said, "...but as for me and my house, we will serve the Lord." Joshua was clearly saying his descendants and family members would worship the only true God, the God of Abraham, Isaac, and Jacob. That is what the man of the family does in his role as the chaplain.

Biblical prophets saw things revealed by God through a voice, a dream, or a vision. But God has given us His finished revelation in His Word. The family chaplain needs to familiarize himself with the Scriptures laid as the foundation for our Christian way of life. He needs to see things today through that biblical lens. Why? Because our world is offering counterfeits and substitutes in place of God-honoring values and lifestyles. To be blunt, the media and the entertainment industry, along with scholastic and educational curriculum, repeatedly tell our children lies, offering them alternative choices, often diametrically opposed to the ways of the Lord and the truths of His Book. Yet through godly leadership, the bad messaging our children, or grandchildren, or their friends have received can be countered with Scripture—God's Word—and also with history. We need to learn about societies that have made bad, unholy cultural choices in the past. That way we'll have an answer for those who seek to justify their present unbiblical behavior.

For example, when your children are being repeatedly told about the virtues of LGBT behaviors or "same-sex marriage is a civil right," what are you going to say to them? Do same-sex behaviors and marriages represent God's vision for His people? A well-informed family chaplain knows enough to say, "Let's talk about this. Because first of all, the Bible is clear about such behavior and second, I don't think you know much about the civil rights era or what a 'civil right' really is."

I was around during the civil rights movement and maybe you were, too. But if not, you'll have to do your homework. That way you're able to say, "OK, I've studied this. So, let me explain to you what the civil rights movement was about. It was about people not being given equal freedoms and opportunities because of the color of their skin. You can explain how those who were deprived of their rights didn't choose to be that color—black, brown, or whatever—any more than some of us turned out to be white. But of this we can be sure; we are all made in the image of God—just the way we are.

With that in mind, is it okay to say those who are involved in homosexual relationships were created that way and therefore they have a "civil right" to do whatever they feel like doing? No, that's not what the Bible teaches us. The Bible frames homosexual behavior as a *choice*—and not a good choice. That *chosen behavior* is not godly, because the Scripture is clear about the sinful nature of homosexuality. By the way, it's no different, and no worse, than the guy who's sleeping with his secretary instead of his wife. It's all sexual sin and it's covered in Romans 1 and elsewhere in the Bible.

Now let me be clear on a couple of things at this point, since I know already that I will be criticized for even raising the issue of homosexuality. First of all, sin is sin, period. I know; I am guilty of committing many of them. Christians need to see homosexuality in the context of all the sins listed in the Bible. Some have greater consequences, but all sin is wrong and separates us from the closeness to God we should be seeking in our lives. If you are a practicing homosexual and I am a fornicator, who has committed the greater sin? Well, I hope you get the point that we are equally sinners. It is all wrong and displeasing to God.

The second point is that while the Supreme Court may have created rights for LGBT couples to marry, that does not mean I am under any mandate to celebrate it. I will not be bullied into compromising on my beliefs about the whole issue of sexual sin or any other kind of sin for that matter. Sin not only breaks God's laws, it breaks His heart. As a spiritual leader of my home, I need to communicate how sin not only grieves God, but it grieves me as well because it hurts all involved.

Take the LGBT-identifying individual—whom God loves by the way, enough to send Jesus to die for him or her—out of the conversation for a moment, and let's focus on the sinful behavior and the oppressive agenda being hammered into our kids and bombarding our culture. Christians who object or resist simply because of their biblical beliefs are being harassed, fined, fired, court-martialed, and even jailed for refusing to submit. What are you going to do about that? Are you going to be a voice of truth in a world that supports the lies of Satan? As the chaplain of the family, you must be clear, both about where you stand and why you believe what you are standing for. By the way, your values ought to impact your vote and your family needs to see that as well.

What about what Christians call "Right to Life"? There's plenty of Scripture that defends life and the family chaplain has to be able to explain that. Yes, we believe in freedom and individual choice. But if somebody killed a person you were close to and said, "Well, I had the right to choose to do that," your anger would bring you to the boiling point. What's the difference?

Right to Life is primarily about babies. And, unbelievably, as I mentioned earlier, today we have states passing laws allowing babies to be euthanized *after birth*. Why doesn't everyone see that as murder? You still think that's a choice? If you can murder a baby a few hours old, why can't you murder one six months old? A year old? Because it has a deformity? Or because of some other perceived deficiency?

As the chaplain, you'll need to be able to explain, both in logical and in biblical terms, why that kind of reasoning is just wrong. If you say "Well, it is just common sense you cannot kill a baby after the child is born," you would be wrong. If it was common sense, we wouldn't have these laws on the books. Remember this—political correctness now trumps common sense.

Again, when you do your civic duty and vote, are you looking for candidates who line up with your values on human life? You should be. There is a very true old saying "Bad politicians are elected by good people who don't vote." I would add that sometimes bad politicians are voted in by good people who did not vote based on their biblical values. Your family should see a consistency between the values you talk about at home and the way you vote.

Bottom line: the chaplain has to know what the Bible says, so he can prepare his family, friends, and colleagues for the turf wars, skirmishes, and all-out conflicts that continue to arise with alarming frequency in today's America—battles against God's ways, battles against truth, and our counter-battles against a culture of destructive behavior and death.

The chaplain and biblical prophecy.

We are indeed living in dark times. And that raises another question. How much do you know about biblical prophecy, about the "signs of the times" signaling the end of this old world, the coming of Christ?

The chaplain should be able to identify some of these signs and the ever-increasing evils in this world today, explain how they portend Jesus's imminent return, and how we need to prepare for it. We don't know—it could be thousands of years from now, but it could also be today or tonight the way I read Scripture. As one old preacher used to say, "I'm not on the planning committee, just on the welcoming committee!" Seriously, we may all be in the presence of Christ in a very short amount of time. (Which means you may not be able to finish this book. Oh well, wouldn't you rather see Jesus face-to-face anyhow?!)

Until that day arrives, I think we can all agree, regardless of our view of end times, it's essential for us to remain alert about what's happening in our world. North Africa and the Middle East are good places to start.

For example, I think we need to see the stage being set for the war of Gog and Magog as prophesied in Ezekiel 38 and 39 that will take place before the end. If you aren't familiar with that passage, please open your Bible and read it right now.

In light of those passages and as current events unfold, I think we should recognize Turkey as a key player in the war of Gog and Magog. I would make the case most of the players in Ezekiel 38 are currently fighting in Syria. Some theologians would likely disagree and would place far more emphasis on Russia than I do. However, I have studied this in some detail and can explain biblically why I believe Turkey is the country to watch closely.

It's essential for the chaplain to be informed about biblical prophecy and to keep up with current events in light of it. Theologian and author Charles R. Peterson stresses this in his book *With Bible in One Hand and Newspaper in the Other.* Peterson highlights how important it is to stay abreast of current events, especially those unfolding in the Middle East and North Africa.

As the chaplain, you've got to know what's going on prophetically and be able to explain it to your family and the people around you. The way to do that is to study carefully. Then you'll be able to point out some of the ancient prophetic passages that seem to be unfolding before our eyes even now. What is the point? To instill a sense of spiritual readiness. Jesus said, "But keep on the alert at all times, praying that you may have strength to escape all these things that are about to take place, and to stand before the Son of Man" (Luke 21:36 [NASB]). The spiritual leader helps his family live with anticipation, hope, and even longing for the coming of the Lord.

Offering a father's blessing

One of the most tragic circumstances our American society is facing is the increasing number of fatherless children. In Matthew 26:31(NIV), the Lord says, "I will strike the shepherd and the sheep will be dispersed." Obviously, that Scripture speaks of what was about to happen to Jesus, but stop and think about those words in relation to what is happening in our culture. The shepherd in every family is the man—the father. He's the one who provides for and protects his flock. And to paraphrase Jesus's words, "I will strike the man, and the family will disperse."

Tragically, that's what's happening in America. Some children are born never knowing who their father is. Others see their daddy pack up and leave while they are still little kids; they grieve for him and miss him terribly. Some fathers are in jail; others are addicted; still others are too busy making money to be bothered with their own sons and daughters. There are so many fatherless families for so many reasons.

In the mass shootings over the recent years in the U.S., if you look at the background of the shooters, you'll find twenty-seven out of twenty-eight of them did not have fathers in their lives. There was only one who did: Adam Lanza at Sandy Hook. The others were fatherless.

We have these kids growing up who have never been affirmed by men in their lives. They've had no man to set a good example, or to help establish values in the home, to love and nurture them. Instead they're raised on the internet and by the violence of video games. If there were fathers present who understood the importance of their role and the power of a father's blessing, I think it would have a huge impact on the tragedies we're facing in today's America. As I'll point out later, a father's blessing opens a pathway to accomplishing the things of God.

That's why a man's role as a chaplain in the family is a God-ordained, spiritual calling.

As the chaplain—and this really applies to grandfathers as well as fathers—during the family gatherings, the whole family needs to see you pray. You'll never get too old to say a prayer at the table. Your son needs to give you that opportunity. It's important for the grandchildren to remember seeing Grandpa pray.

At Christmastime, the elder patriarch needs to be the one to read the Christmas story. At Easter, he needs to be the one to share the Bible passages about the death and resurrection of Jesus. It's important because he is imparting to the rest of the family that he recognizes, accepts, and is willing to execute his rightful role.

You may say, "I don't know the Scriptures that well." Okay, good. At least you recognize that! Now go read the Bible or listen to a recording of it. "Faith comes from hearing, and hearing by the word of Christ" (Rom. 10:17 [NASB]).

One of a chaplain's primary responsibilities is to give the father's blessing to his children and his wife. "Blessing" is the opposite of a "curse." I'm afraid many more men curse their wives than bless them. How do you curse her? Either with literal profanity, or neglect, or abuse, or any number of ways women are cursed by their husbands, who are supposed to be the chaplains, priests, or pastors—the representatives of Christ in the family.

It bears repeating you are not and cannot be a perfect man without flaws. But most of us can do better than we have done in the past regarding how we treat our wives.

One of the principles to keep in mind is a blessing has to be spoken. It's not just a blessing silently offered during a time of private prayer. There is authority in the spoken word, and power in the tongue—for good and for evil. We have to remember blessings come from the heart and mind, but then through the vocal cords and lips of the one giving the blessing.

In fact, there is a blessing spoken in the first chapter of the first book of the Bible—a blessing on Adam and Eve. Genesis 1:27 (NIV): "So God created man in his own image, in the image of God he created them, male and female…" And then in verse 28, what was the first thing he did after he created them? "God blessed them." At the very beginning, the power of the blessing was revealed by God.

In Hebrews 11:20 (NKJV), the writer says, "By faith, Isaac blessed Jacob concerning things to come." Verse 21 goes on to say, "By faith, Jacob, when he was dying, blessed each of the sons of Joseph, and worshipped, leaning on the top of his staff."

Hebrews 11 is a powerful and beautiful chapter of God's Word recounting blessings and wonders that took place through the faith of the earliest patriarchs and other biblical characters. We need to understand the power of the spoken word, of the blessing, of the affirmation.

One of the major problems with America's absentee fathers is we've got all these young boys and girls who have never had the affirmation of their patriarchy. There was no old grandpa who put those kids on his knee and told them how much he loved them. No one said, "I'm so proud of you. You're my flesh and blood and I have great expectations for you." By blessing your children, your grandchildren, and other boys and girls who have no father, you can help defeat the hopelessness we see in communities today because of absentee fathers.

Of course, the person receiving the blessing—son, daughter, wife—has to make certain choices in life in order for God's will to be fulfilled. That spoken word opens a new path for them. Remember, it's not an earned reward, but rather part of each person's identity. It's not about whether we deserve it or whether we're without flaws or saved or unsaved; it's about the responsibility of the patriarch to declare the father's blessing no matter what. I believe the father's blessing can open the pathway to salvation.

The emotion associated with the experience alone can start them thinking. When you lay your hands on someone, and bless and affirm them, you are giving the Holy Spirit a better opportunity to speak into their mind and draw them to Christ. It's not an end-all, but it helps prepare the way. That blessing also looks beyond today and sees the future.

My father came to Christ late in life, so he never understood the significance and importance of the father's blessing. Simply stated, he never blessed me. As I matured in my Christian life, I began to realize how important that blessing is, and I yearned for what I knew I could never have because the opportunity for that affirmation died when my dad went to be with the Lord on July 7th, 2001.

As I traveled around the country conducting men's conferences, I always ended the conference by asking men to bring their sons to the altar, lay their hands on them and bless them. One night I was speaking in Katy, Texas, to a large international group of men. As I asked the men and their sons to come forward, I mentioned that one of my great regrets in life was that my dad never blessed me; he never affirmed me as a man.

Men and their sons began to move toward the stage at this out-door event, and I noticed a man with no son moving toward me. I wasn't sure why, but I could just tell from his countenance he was following the prompting of the Holy Spirit in whatever he was doing. Then this very muscular black man stepped up directly in front of me, looked directly into my eyes, and said in a very comforting way, "I am Pastor Charles Flowers from San Antonio. If you will allow me, I will give you the Father's blessing on behalf of your deceased father."

My eyes filled with tears as he blessed and affirmed me. It was one of the most emotional moments of my life, as Pastor Flowers placed his hands on my head and spoke blessings on me. I cannot adequately describe the impact this one event had on my ministry. From that point on I ended men's conferences with the church pastor and other men of authority providing that same blessing to every man who would come forward to receive it. I'll just say I have personally felt the power of a man in authority laying his hands on me, blessing and affirming me. And I have no doubt that many men's lives would be changed if they could receive exactly what I received that night in Katy.

What does that blessing say? There is no single template for it. Just say what you would want said to you. Here is a sample but only an example because many things are appropriate.

"I bless and affirm you as my child, as someone who God loves and has a plan for. I have great hopes for you. May you be prolific. May you multiply and produce offspring of which I can also be proud and who God can use. I bless you!"

Or in the case of your wife: "I bless you as my wife and helpmate. I affirm you as a virtuous woman who has made me a complete man. I bless you as the mother of my offspring and a woman I love as Christ loved the church."

When you bestow the father's blessing, it instills in those you've blessed a sense of parental or marital acceptance. "I accept you just as you are. I don't accept your behavior sometimes, but I accept you because you're my flesh and blood—or you're grafted in—and I've made you part of my family."

So many children are rejected today, one way or another. What a powerful thing it is when those we bless are made to feel accepted and blessed. And how overwhelming it is to realize God wants to bless us all. The last chapter of Deuteronomy tells us Joshua was "full of the Spirit of Wisdom for Moses had laid his hands on him" (Deut. 34:9 [NKJV]). In other words, Moses prayed blessings over Joshua.

If it was good for Joshua, then it should be good for us today. I pray you'll bless your family so they too may be filled with the Spirit and ready to do battle as Joshua was.

Man as a Chaplain—
A Word for Women

Who are the main men in your life? Your sons, your brothers, your fiancé, boyfriend, or husband? In every case, building strong relationships based on God's Word and His presence provides the safest and most secure foundation possible. I hope you'll encourage those special boys and men you love so much to become strong leaders in the home as well as at school, work, or wherever they find themselves in the future.

What can you and your husband do to nurture your spirituality? For families, reading the Bible or a devotional book and praying together as the day begins is a "holy habit" that can strengthen and encourage all concerned. And if you're the mother of children, just as General Boykin has described a "father's blessing" and its importance for male-to-male empowerment, as a mother and wife, you too can bless your husband and your boys, as well as the daughters in your life. If you were to write a "mother's blessing" or a "wife's blessing," what would it say?

In times of trouble, your offering of encouragement based on faith and trust in God can provide great comfort in the midst of disappointing circumstances. In fact, you and your husband need to encourage one another, which sometimes requires extra efforts at communication. Before you need it, give some thought to ways you can create an atmosphere of healing, forgiveness, and a "fresh start" together.

Encouraging your husband to serve as the chaplain in your home will strengthen him as well as you and the children. Everyday family routines, centered around God's Word and prayer, will bless all of you for a lifetime.

MAN AS A CHAPLAIN—
DISCUSSION QUESTIONS

1. As the Chaplain, you are to set the spiritual climate within your home. What do you want the spiritual climate in your home to look like? Be specific. How can you achieve this? Write out a plan.

2. As the spiritual leader and head of the home, Dad must often make personal sacrifices, following the model of Jesus (Eph. 5:25). Can you think of any personal sacrifices you have made or should be making for your kids and wife? If you don't have a family of your own yet, can you think of what sacrifices you may need to make once you do?

3. As the family chaplain, you are also meant to provide vision. Have you asked God to give you vision for your family? If so, what is it God may be calling you and your family to in the days and years ahead? If not, what might be getting in the way of you hearing God's vision and how can you be seeking that vision?

4. Once you have sought and received vision for your family, pray it over, think it through, and write it down. Then you need to communicate it in a clear and compelling way. What are some specific ways you can provide your wife and kids with direction toward realizing that vision?

5. You were encouraged to see things in life through a biblical lens, but the first step is familiarity with the Scriptures. Rate yourself, one to ten, on general Bible knowledge. What steps can you take to get a better handle on the Bible?

6. How can you help your family see things in life through a biblical lens?

7. As the chaplain, you need to be able to explain, both in common sense and in biblical terms, why certain things like same-sex marriage and abortion are wrong. How would you explain this to your family if they were sitting with you right now?

8. The chaplain has a prophetic role of identifying the signs of the times, seeing how they line up with biblical prophecy, and how they portend that Jesus's return is imminent. Can you identify a few of these, right now, and how you think they point to how we are moving closer to Jesus's return?

9. One of the most tragic circumstances our American society is facing is the increasing number of fatherless children. It is important for children to have present fathers in their lives. This means not just living with them but actually being involved in their lives. If you have children, or plan to, how can you be more present in their lives?

10. Have you spoken a blessing over your wife and kids? If not, start by trying to come up with something you can say in a blessing over them—what would it involve? Again, pray it over, think it through, and write it down. Then make plans to confer this blessing on a special day in the life of that family member or plan to do it as a group.

CHAPTER SIX

FINISH STRONG

I firmly believe that any man's finest hour, the greatest fulfillment of all that he holds dear, is that moment when he has worked his heart out in a good cause and lies exhausted on the field of battle—victorious.

—Vince Lombardi

For though we live in the world, we do not wage war as the world does. The weapons we fight with are not the weapons of the world. On the contrary, they have divine power to demolish strongholds. We demolish arguments and every pretension that sets itself up against the

knowledge of God, and we take captive every thought to
make it obedient to Christ.

—2 Corinthians 10:3–5 (NIV)

Perhaps after reading what I've written in the previous pages, you're wondering what to do next. You may see yourself as a man who has, in one way or another, failed to do the things God has expected of you. If so, I hope you'll do what we all have to do now and then—stand, face your failure, then try to get it right going forward.

I have never been all God wanted me to be. In fact, if the Father can be disappointed, I'm sure I've given Him reason. Simply stated, I have failed at different times. (Since my wife is reading this book, let me just add, no, sweetheart, that has not been one of my failures. But you already knew that.) But I am intent on doing better and getting closer to becoming the man I need to be. You should do the same, and I hope you'll put the past behind you. And pray for wisdom, courage, and understanding.

Maybe the thing most important for you to understand is you are in a battle. The moment you accept Christ as your Savior, you are assured of three key things:

First—God will never leave you nor forsake you.
Second—Your place in Heaven is assured.
Third—From now on you're going to be in a
spiritual battle.

There isn't enough focus today on spiritual warfare, either in the church or in the Christian world. Consequently, many Christians are unprepared for the schemes of our adversary. To be the men God has called us to be, we have to anticipate that conflicts lie ahead. Get ready, prepare yourself, and armor up because spiritual warfare is real, and our adversary Satan is on the prowl. In fact, he is coming for you. But don't be intimidated or afraid because God has given each of us all we need to be victorious. "Greater is he that is in you, than he that is in the world" (1 John 4:4 [KJV]).

I never went into a physical battle without putting on my "battle rattle"—my gear and my weapons. In the same way, we all need to armor up for our spiritual battles.

Armed for warfare

In his 2004 book *A Table in the Presence*, Lieutenant Carey Cash—a Navy chaplain serving with U.S. Marines—describes the spiritual, and military, preparations he and his troops made before going into combat in Iraq on March 20, 2003.

> For forty days the men of First Battalion, Fifth Marine regiment, camped in the desert of northern Kuwait and prepared themselves for war. Forty days in the wilderness—a duration of biblical proportions. The days were long, and the wind was merciless. The nights were cold, and the sky was always alight

with the glow of distant fires burning in a dangerous land. And yet, in that vast, desolate and inhospitable setting, the ache of loneliness and uncertainty became the blessing of solitude and spiritual hunger…

…Only days before we would witness the terrors of war, forty-nine Marines and sailors gathered together before the eyes of the entire camp. Professing their new-found faith, they were baptized into the kingdom of God as new Christians…

On March 20, we were twenty miles north…the men of Alpha Company had just crossed into Iraq. Twelve AAVs and three M-1 Abrams tanks crept slowly along, each driver's eyes constantly checking his forward, flanks, and rear for any sign of the enemy. Our own artillery fire was still lighting up the sky as steel Marine Corps beasts churned through the sand and sediment of the desert. The evening was cool and damp, but the inside of each swaying AAV was stifling hot, crammed with twenty-five Marines in combat gear, squeezed into a space no bigger than a dentist's office lobby. Sweat dripped down their foreheads. They shifted continually, adjusting themselves, checking and rechecking their gear, making sure they had everything they needed—ammo magazines, grenades, water, night-vision goggles, crosses, prayer cards. They gripped their fully loaded rifles and more than a few of them prayed. There was no turning back.

Those sailors and marines who spent forty days in Kuwait spent many more months at Camp Pendleton, California, preparing for the enemy they were about to engage. They were as prepared as they'd ever be when they finally rolled across Iraq's border. They checked, double-checked, and triple-checked their weapons, knowing very well some of them wouldn't return alive. Certainly not one of them took his situation lightly.

We Christians have been assured there's a battle raging around us right now and we're going to need the weapons we've been given, whether we are looking forward to using them or not.

The Apostle Paul instructs us in Ephesians 6 to "Put on the whole armor of God" and several of our weapons—offensive and defensive—have been identified. It's one of my favorite Scriptures because I have an affinity for things related to warfare. Despite the great success of Rome's fabled warriors, it's been about 2,000 years since the specific weapons cited in Paul's instructions have been put to use. So, as we prepare for the conflicts we'll surely face as Christians, it's good for us to read Paul's instructions and then give some thought to what those weapons are meant to do.

The first thing we have to understand—even before reading that Ephesians passage—is another piece of advice, this one written by Peter. He said, "Be sober, be vigilant; because your adversary the devil, as a roaring lion, walketh about, seeking whom he may devour" (1 Pet. 5:8 [KJV]).

What he's saying is our adversary is Satan. Then we read Paul's words (Eph. 6:10-18 [NIV]), where he describes what comprises the whole armor of God.:

> Finally, be strong in the Lord and in his mighty power. Put on the full armor of God, so that you can take your stand against the devil's schemes. For our struggle is not against flesh and blood, but against the rulers, against the authorities, against the powers of this dark world and against the spiritual forces of evil in the heavenly realms. Therefore, put on the full armor of God, so that when the day of evil comes, you may be able to stand your ground, and after you have done everything, to stand. Stand firm then, with the belt of truth buckled around your waist, with the breastplate of righteousness in place, and with your feet fitted with the readiness that comes from the gospel of peace. In addition to all this, take up the shield of faith, with which you can extinguish all the flaming arrows of the evil one. Take the helmet of salvation and the sword of the Spirit, which is the word of God.
>
> And pray in the Spirit on all occasions with all kinds of prayers and requests. With this in mind,

be alert and always keep on praying for all the
Lord's people.

In so many words, Paul warns us, "Put the armor on and keep it
on. Don't take it off. You don't just put it on when you're planning
to go into battle. You have to recognize you're in the battle every
single day."

Let me repeat, there's not enough preaching or teaching about the
reality of the spiritual war we're in. And there are many Christians all
around us who really are "saved," but they don't understand that once
they have received Christ into their lives, they have entered a battle.
That's why so many believers are not prepared to fight. Instead of
training themselves for the next firefight, they're dwelling on remorse
for their bad choices or for wrong things they've said or done, or
they're thinking maybe their foolishness has brought this trouble
down on them. They haven't yet realized they're in a battle and, in
a way, they've already been wounded, thanks to their lack of understanding of God's grace.

Paul gives us explicit instructions about preparing for war and
describes how we should put on the whole armor of God. He began
with the belt of truth. Paul was very familiar with Roman soldiers—
he was surrounded by them. As he wrote about the belt of truth,
he was reflecting on the way those soldiers went into battle having
"girded their loins." This unusual belt, which the Romans called a
balteus, was necessary because in those days men wore robes and
couldn't fight effectively in them. So, they would gather up the fabric

of the robe, tuck it into their groin area, and pull up straps between their legs, attaching them on the sides and the back of the belt. This would not only hold their garments in place, but it would protect a sensitive part of the body. The whole idea was to put on that belt so they could fight.

Paul speaks of it as the belt of truth and where does truth come from? Jesus said He is the "Way, the Truth, and the Life." Meanwhile, every lie can be traced back to Satan.

An obvious example of one of today's biggest lies, one that clearly hurts so many people in this confused world, is this: if you're born with male genitalia, you can become a woman instead. And, perhaps even more perversely, the same with a female. It's not common sense, but some people seem to have left common sense behind them some time ago. In fact, political correctness has replaced truth. Only by going back to the Word of God—studying it and being adept at remembering the Scriptures—are we going to understand truth. The belt of truth Paul is talking about is biblical truth.

Gird your loins with the belt of truth. Know what you believe and why. It's not good enough to believe something because someone said it to you. You've got to recognize the difference between true and false, and remember Satan is the author of lies. Jesus Christ is the ultimate Truth and all Truths emanate from Him.

How can you find the Truth about some specific concern? First, pray and ask God for revelation, to lead you to Scripture. It's amazing how, once we ask, even after we've been leafing through the Bible aimlessly, suddenly there's our answer, and it's right in front of us!

Why didn't we see it before? Because we weren't looking for it and we hadn't asked.

When Jesus was led into the wilderness, he responded to Satan's offers every time with a simple statement. "It is written…." Because Jesus is the Word, when Satan tried to sabotage his sinlessness, He could simply say, "It is written…" Satan left defeated. You can beat him too. James 4:7 (NKJV) says, "[S]ubmit to God. Resist the devil and he will flee from you." How do you resist the devil and his temptations? Cinch up that belt of truth.

The breastplate of righteousness was the second thing Paul introduced. The Roman breastplate, or *lorica segmentata*, which was a segmented armor, was constructed of strips of iron joined with hooks or leather straps. It covered the chest and shoulders down to the waist and was meant to fend off spears, arrows, and swords. This all served to protect the heart and other vital organs. In Hebrew thinking, the heart was the seat of the mind and the will, while the intestines or bowels were the seat of the emotions. Consequently, the breastplate of righteousness protects the believer's mind, will, and emotions, which are often subject to attack by Satan.

The U.S. Army has spent a considerable amount of money developing body armor. Not only do soldiers have a Kevlar vest, but there is also a high-density ceramic plate, weighing about thirty pounds, that slides into a pocket. The combination stops the bullets of the enemy and saves lives. In fact, one of my men took a round from an AK-47 in the lower back but it didn't penetrate. When he took off his gear, he had a nasty bruise and his urine was bloody for a week, but he lived to fight another day. I've seen men who have taken a hit and walked away because that body armor protected them. We need to put on that breastplate of righteousness.

Sometimes people hear about this breastplate and they say, "Well, I'm not righteous." And my response is that is a contradiction of the Word of God because "God made him who had no sin to be sin for us, so that in him we might become the righteousness of God" (2 Cor. 5:21 [NIV]). Yes, it's amazing, but we really are made righteous, positionally, in Christ when we respond to the Gospel and accept Christ as our redeemer and are saved.

What does that mean to you and me on a daily basis? Well even though we've been made righteous through Christ's blood, we still have to fight a daily battle to remain pure. Again, the breastplate covers a very important part of our body—our heart. That's why we read in Proverbs 4:23 (NIV), "Above all else, guard your heart, for everything you do flows from it." Interestingly, an earlier version of the Roman breastplate was called the *pectorale*, which literally means "heart-guard," because it covered only about eight inches over the heart. We need to guard our hearts and His righteousness makes that possible.

By the way, don't make the mistake of thinking you can march along the margins of evil—if you try that you're going to get trapped in it. Don't imagine you can have a taste of sin without getting swallowed up by it. *Guard your heart.* In what ways are you vulnerable? Ask God specifically for help. Seek prayer and intercession from others—people who are willing to say, "I will pray for you. I will intercede for you."

Paul's next piece of armor was footwear—we are to have our feet fitted with "the readiness that comes from the gospel of peace" (Eph. 6:19 [NIV]). You've probably heard the old saying "An army marches on its stomach." Figuratively speaking, Napoleon had it right, but literally, the infantry marches in boots. Sturdy footgear for the warrior is as important today as it was back when Paul wrote this. The Roman soldier had thick, metal-studded soles on his leather-strapped footgear called *caligae*. These open, hob-nailed boots provided stability when marching through tough terrain and engaging in hand-to-hand combat with the enemy. We need to be able to plant our feet firmly in anticipation of the devil's assault. But there is still more here. There is peace in the midst of battle.

In Galatians 5:22 (NIV), we learn peace is one of several wonderful blessings we receive from the Holy Spirit. "The fruit of the Spirit is love, joy, *peace*, forbearance, kindness, goodness, faithfulness." If we are redeemed, we should have peace in our soul about where we will spend eternity. We have to accept the fact Jesus washed away all our sins (1 John, 1:9 [NIV]). That's a promise and we not only need to believe it but thank Him for it.

Guilty feelings can rob us of our peace. Every time you have a temptation, that desire alone does not mean you've sinned. Every time you have a fleeting thought doesn't mean you've transgressed, unless you start to develop that thought. The fact it came into your mind means you have a carnal nature suppressed by the blood of

Jesus. We just have to make sure the Gospel is an essential part of our lives. It will bring us peace, and we'll know Jesus Christ resides within us. In Hebrew, "peace," or *shalom,* is the same word as "oneness" or "completeness." And "gospel" translates to "good news." The good news of our oneness with Christ brings peace to our souls. Our feet are anchored in peace because of the Gospel.

That peace also should give us the confidence to share our faith. What does sharing our faith have to do with spiritual warfare? Everything! Sharing the Gospel with someone who then repents of his sin, puts his trust in Christ as Savior, and follows Him as Lord liberates one of the devil's captives. Put on those boots and boldly tell others about the gospel of peace found in Jesus!

The next thing Paul tells us about is the shield of faith. The Roman shield, or *scutum,* was constructed out of wood planks, covered with canvas and stretched leather. Rectangular and semicylindrical in shape, the Roman shield was an imposing piece of armor, roughly four feet tall and two feet wide. Given the fact an average recruit had to be five feet, five inches tall, the coverage of this shield was a substantial defense against sword, spear, and arrow.

Men, you need to "hold up" the shield of faith (see the New Living Translation of Ephesians 6:16). Make no mistake, the devil is gunning for you. He has you in his sights. Don't give him any help by dropping your shield. One time I said to my dear praying mother, "Mom, I'll tell you one thing. The one thing Satan will never trick me into is betraying my wife by committing adultery." My sweet mom who does not have a high school education looked at me and asked, "Are you stupid?!" I backed up and sheepishly asked, "What do you mean?" She said, "You just told Satan exactly where to attack you!" Oh, man, she was right. I just gave the devil vital intel he could exploit. She told me to rebuke it and I did. I learned from my mistake. I had momentarily dropped by shield.

As a defensive weapon, the Roman shield was often soaked in water before battle, which extinguished incoming fiery darts. Dip your shield daily in the Word and ask God to increase your faith and to help you extinguish the fiery darts of the enemy. Keep that shield up!

However, the shield is one of the few things in the list of armor that is both a defensive and an offensive weapon. Most historians won't tell you, but a warrior would actually use his shield to ram the enemy, knocking him back and off-balance so he could get his sword into him. Notice it is the shield of "faith." Your faith in, trust in, and dependence on Almighty God is key to victory. Don't just take my word for it. No less than the Apostle John, the beloved disciple, declared, "This is the victory that has overcome the world, even our faith. Who is it that overcomes the world? Only the one who believes that Jesus is the Son of God" (1 John 5:4b-5 [NIV]).

Jesus, the object of our faith, empowers us to overcome the enemy and gain the victory. The shield could be used on offense. Take that shield of faith and break the devil's jaw, soldier! Yeah, I know what some of you are thinking: "I struggle with my faith sometimes. At times I even question whether God is even real." Well here is my response: "Welcome to the real world." Even Mother Teresa admitted to struggling with her faith at times. Those periods of doubt are when you rely on your knowledge of the Scriptures and not on your emotions. Just keep asking God for a renewed faith.

If you have read my autobiography, *Never Surrender*, you know, as I described in a previous chapter, I actually sat on my bunk and denied the very existence of God as I grieved for fifteen soldiers who died the day before in the Black Hawk Down battle. Yes, I temporarily lost my faith but as I have already explained, I snapped back when I heard the voice of the Lord and felt His presence. Let me remind you we are all still humans and more importantly, we are all in a raging battle. Try to grow every day in your faith by dipping that shield in the water of the word and through your prayer life.

Next Paul tells us to take hold of the helmet of salvation. That iconic Roman helmet, or *galea,* with its drop-down cheek and neck guards, was often made of either beaten bronze or iron. However, some officers were issued hardened steel helmets. In the U.S. Army, we began using general-issue helmets during World War I. Remember the "doughboys," as they called them, with their steel helmets that flared out at the ears? Well they didn't protect you from a bullet, maybe some shrapnel. Then in World War II, they were upgraded to be somewhat more protective. But in the 1980s, the army developed ballistic helmets, so the ones we use today will deflect most small-arms rifle rounds and protect you. In fact, a soldier right next to me was shot in the head with an AK round, but his helmet protected him. He was goofy for the next two weeks, but he was alive to tell about it. Just as the breastplate protects the heart, the helmet of salvation obviously protects the head. More on that in a moment.

Why did Paul put the helmet last on his list of defensive armor? He obviously watched Roman soldiers put on their armor and they put their helmets on last. For the believer, salvation is the first thing. Interestingly, the verb here can mean "to receive" the helmet. Certainly, salvation is a gift we receive by faith in Christ, as Paul tells us earlier in Ephesians 2:8-9. While salvation comes the moment we place our trust in Christ's death, resurrection, and payment of sin, it is a process.

We're saved and then we grow daily by drawing closer to him through faith and obedience, which is what the Bible calls sanctification. However, anybody who thinks our spiritual life is a straight, vertical climb is not being realistic. Mine has zigzags in it, and I've had a few setbacks. As the old saying goes, sometimes it has been one step forward, two steps back. We'll eventually get there by the time we draw our last breath. But this holy helmet reinforces the fact we've got to be redeemed by Christ's blood and then we can continue to grow in our sanctification process, with his help.

Back to the purpose of the helmet—the helmet of salvation is protection for the mind. The mind is the primary site for spiritual warfare, so we've got to protect it. How do we do that? You would never pick dog droppings up off the ground and ingest them into your body. Yet we sometimes ingest things through our minds by way of our senses—through our ears and especially our eyes. What do we ingest through our eyes that helps to destroy us, making that war in our minds rage? Pornography. As we've seen, for so many men—most men according to the statistics—it is our secret weakness. That's why pornography is so dangerous; we won't pick up filth off the ground, but we'll ingest it through our eyes. Once in, it takes over our minds, it strangles our hearts toward our wives, and it poisons our souls. Like a cancer, it's killing us. It's killing our families.

As Paul urges in Romans 12:2 (NASB), "And do not be conformed to this world, but be transformed by the renewing of your mind, so that you may prove what the will of God is, that which is good and acceptable and perfect." Men, guard your mind by putting on your helmet!

Then Paul finally tells us to take the sword of the Spirit, which is the word of God (verse 17). The Roman sword, or *gladius,* from which we get the word "gladiator," was not like the long broadsword you saw in the movie *Braveheart.* It was shorter, typically between twenty-four and thirty-three inches in length. This sword was double-edged. In fact, the book of Hebrews makes the same comparison Paul does here: "For the word of God is living and active and sharper than any two-edged sword, and piercing as far as the division of soul and spirit, of both joints and marrow, and able to judge the thoughts and intentions of the heart" (Heb. 4:12 [NASB]).

We use the word to encourage our hearts, strengthen our faith, combat temptation, share the Gospel, and defeat the enemy. Again, a common theme in all of these weapons is the word of God. What does that mean? To take up the sword of the Spirit? For me, it means going on the offense. With some exceptions, the other items of armor are mostly defensive in nature, but this one is used for attack. In fact, notice there really is no defensive armor mentioned for the backside. That means no retreat. Men, move forward! Swing that sword!

What is the purpose, the mission? Right after Jesus defeated the devil in the wilderness with the Word of God, He declared his mission was to "proclaim liberty to captives" and "set at liberty those oppressed" in Luke 4:18-19 (NKJV). Christ came as a liberator of the oppressed. The Latin motto for the U.S. Army Green Berets could have come right out of that passage—*De oppresso liber*—to "free the oppressed." I had the privilege of commanding that elite group of warriors, some ten thousand strong.

In World War II, British Prime Minister Winston Churchill and President Franklin Delano Roosevelt decided to form the Office of Strategic Services (OSS). The plan was to deploy three-man teams to drop behind enemy lines in occupied territory to degrade Nazi forces by any means necessary with the ultimate goal of freeing the oppressed people. After the war, the U.S. Army continued that strategic approach through the Green Berets, launched in 1952. They have an incredibly high causality rate because they are on the front lines. These men are some of the finest warriors who have ever served in the military. The mission of the Green Berets is to "free the oppressed."

In spiritual warfare, we must use the sword of the Spirit and the Word of God to liberate people from the oppression of the enemy of our souls, to push back the darkness in our culture and reclaim territory from the devil.

Back to your offensive weapon—to wield the Word effectively, we must familiarize ourselves with our weapon. In the army, we were expected to become familiar with our weapon by regular "field stripping," which is basically disassembling the firearm into major component groups so they can be cleaned easily. We became so proficient in field stripping our weapon we could disassemble it and reassemble it in our sleep. We need that kind of familiarity with the Word if we want to wield it effectively.

What does that mean practically? Well we need an active plan for reading, studying, meditating, and applying the Bible to our daily experiences. How are we going to absorb it to become second nature? How do we "field strip" the Word? Beyond reading, studying, and meditating, we'll need something to break it down to a basic level and help us understand it. Obviously, there are confusing passages and chapters in the Bible that cause us to struggle, and we need assistance. It bears repeating—get a good commentary or study guide; find some good online help. If you don't know where to start, ask your pastor, or a seasoned battle buddy, for help. Consider getting involved in a Bible study, where you can actually discuss the meaning of Scripture and the intent of the authors.

Speaking of that battle buddy, get with him, draw swords, and practice using them. No, I'm not taking about a mock sword fight. I'm talking about you taking your Bible and him taking his Bible and you guys drilling down on a passage and discussing it, maybe even debating it. The Bible says, "As iron sharpens iron, so one man sharpens another" (Prov. 27:17 [NASB]). Practice using your sword in that controlled environment with your battle buddy before waging war with the enemy.

That's why my men in Special Forces spend so much time on the range, firing their weapons to gain proficiency and accuracy. Then they're placed in teams to run close-quarter battles (CQB) and other scenarios to learn tactics and teamwork that will dislodge and defeat the enemy effectively. When the moment comes and you find yourself in a live firefight with the devil and you engage in spiritual warfare, claim the promise I have clung to many times when going into battle, "No weapon formed against you shall prosper" (Isa. 54:17 [NKJV]). Men, take up the sword of the Spirit and fight to win!

Paul's final word about our battle is we should pray. Don't skip this. Success or failure in spiritual warfare depends on it. Pray always. Pray without ceasing. In the final analysis, Paul says, "And pray in the Spirit on all occasions with all kinds of prayers and requests. With this in mind, be alert and always keep on praying for all the Lord's people" (Eph. 6:18 [NIV]).

Power of a ten-second prayer

In the previous chapter, I began relating my experience in the Delta Force operation to free the American hostages in Iran. Here is the rest of that story as it played out in the desert on April 24, 1980. We were at a refueling stop before we were to make our final assault on the embassy to liberate fifty-two of our own from radical Islamists, but our hopes turned to disappointment and desperation as we watched the pilot of a U.S. Navy RH-53 helicopter crash into the U.S. Air Force C-130 carrying forty-five Delta Force members. The helo pilot was refueling from the C-130, but as he attempted to reposition his aircraft, he lost his equilibrium—he "went vertigo," in aviation lingo. Lifting off, he lost control and crashed onto the C-130, slamming into the top and left side of the cargo plane. The eruption was immediate; aviation fuel exploded in the helo and engulfed the C-130 in a massive ball of high-octane fire.

I was walking towards that C-130 to get a head count when the crash occurred. Initially I turned to run as I felt the heat and saw pieces of metal flying out into the desert. But I didn't go far, only a few steps, before I became fully aware of the presence of the Holy Spirit. I even sensed Him calling me to stop and turn back toward the wreckage. I spun around, knowing an explosion would come quickly when the fuel in the C-130 ignited. Then the reality hit me—forty-five Delta Force men were trapped inside the wreckage with no way out and no chance to survive the fire. And I could not help them.

Remember, only eighteen hours earlier I stood with these men in that old Russian MiG base in Wadi Qena, Egypt, as we prayed for God to go with us on this mission. I'd led the prayer that morning before we launched the operation, petitioning God to keep His hand of protection upon us. Now I was watching those same men die a fiery death while I stood by helplessly.

It took only seconds before I instinctively began pleading with God for the lives of these men. My prayer was that of a desperate man who knew only God could save those forty-five souls in that wreckage. "Oh God," I pleaded, "Please spare them! They trusted You, Lord! In Jesus's name, bring them out alive. God, I'm asking You not to let these men die."

It was all I could do—and the most important thing I could do. My plea was sincere. They needed a miracle, and there was no time for a great oration or for promises of what I would do in return if God would come through for them. There wasn't even time for me to go through my normal routine of thanking God for everything He'd already done for me in the past, or for telling Him what a worthless sinner I was—as if He didn't know. And no time for pomp or style or fancy words. Those men needed this miracle now.

There it was, my ten-second prayer. And it was all I had to offer. "Over to You now, God."

Suddenly the right troop door of that C-130 opened. I could barely see through the flames, but instantly I saw the miracle take shape. Forty-five men jumped one by one through those flames and out onto the desert floor and ran from the crash like a redbone hound on the scent of a raccoon. "Yes, Lord—thank You, Lord! You are so awesome, God!" I spoke the words aloud as I ran to greet those men and to help direct them to the other airplanes still on the ground. Never underestimate the power of God in response to a short, simple, sincere prayer.

As the chaplain in your home, among your friends, and in your sphere of influence, prayer may well be the only thing as well as the most important thing you can do. Pray always, watching with perseverance. Remember there is never a bad time to pray. Do you have a prayer list? If not, write down a list of the people you want to pray for daily. A lot of us wind up praying at the end of the day and by then we're fighting sleep. Sometimes my last prayer of the day is to say to God, "Lord, you see this piece of paper I have in my hand, and I'm asking you to meet each need I've listed on it. And please bring a special blessing to every person whose name I've written here."

And may God bless you, too, as you seek to become the man He created you to be. May he make you a generous Provider, a wise Instructor, a courageous Defender, a trustworthy Battle Buddy and a faithful Chaplain. I bless you and I thank God for you.

And I pray you'll Finish Strong!

Finish Strong—
Words for Women

When it comes to spiritual warfare, the word for women is precisely the same as God's Word for men. Although we may face different temptations, we all encounter the same spiritual dangers, risks, and threats. And the Armor of God—spiritual protection against the attacks of our greatest enemy, Satan—is indispensable for us all. We've read what General Boykin writes about spiritual warfare in this chapter.

Have you ever had the sense you were in the midst of a spiritual attack? At some point, do you recall thinking that perhaps some kind of spiritual warfare was going on all around you? At what point did you recognize it, and how did you react? Here are some possibilities and how the weapons of our warfare can be put to good use.

Maybe a false accusation has been made against you. Or perhaps lies are being spread about you or someone you love. Or you may have the feeling that way too many things are all going wrong at the same time. If so, grasping and holding onto the truth—what's *really* going on here?—can become an essential and immediate protective weapon. We need to wrap God's belt of truth around ourselves while we pray.

Sometimes spiritual attacks can take the form of emotional vulnerability—a shadowy depression or anxiety is intruding upon us, perhaps, seemingly for no real reason. By seeking peace in prayer and in a spirit of thanksgiving, the Peace of God will help dispel those spiritual clouds and prepare us to walk forward with firm footing toward better days ahead.

Has your heart ever felt like it's been broken? Is a heartache overwhelming you? The breastplate of righteousness protects our hearts from permanent damage. And it bears repeating—that righteousness isn't about our own goodness or holiness—most of us aren't nearly as righteous as we'd like to be. Instead, we're protected by the righteousness of Jesus, which He provides as a gift to all who put their trust in Him.

Sudden health issues, a betrayal by a friend, or some other unexpected bad news can strike us without warning, like a barrage of flaming arrows. These are things our shield of faith can extinguish before our spirits are injured. Our faith in Him and His power can extinguish the flames.

Likewise, our minds are protected by the helmet of salvation from dangerous thoughts, fears, and other unworthy temptations that may come into our heads from time to time. Our salvation provides God's protection for our minds. But we do need to remember to put the helmet on!

One of our best defenses against temptations, distressing circumstances, and spiritual assaults is the sword of the Spirit—God's Word, the Bible. This is the weapon Jesus used repeatedly during his temptation. And it's just as available to us today as it was to Him.

Finally, the Bible's description of our spiritual armor concludes with this instruction, "Pray in the Spirit on all occasions with all kinds of prayers and requests. With this in mind, be alert and always keep on praying for all the saints."

So pray for all those you cherish and especially for the boys and men in your life. They are facing intense challenges from a very dishonest and destructive culture. Your grace, kindness, and faith—and most of all your prayers—will strengthen them and give them faith and courage to become the men of God He created them to be.

FINISH STRONG—
DISCUSSION QUESTIONS

1. To be the men God has called us to be, we should take a personal inventory on a regular basis. As you look back across your life, what have you left unresolved with God? Confess it, ask God's forgiveness, receive it with thanks, and resolve to move on with his assurance of your salvation.

2. We are instructed to keep the armor of God on every day. Can you give some specific examples of what that should look like in your life? What are some specific ways you can prepare yourself to face inevitable battles?

3. Many Christians haven't realized yet they are in a spiritual battle. Can you give some specific examples of things in our daily lives and society we should be more cautious of? What are some of the clear signs of spiritual warfare?

4. The first piece of armor Paul mentions is the belt of truth. You already read one example of one of today's biggest lies. Can you think of another? How can you put on the belt of truth and combat that lie?

5. The second piece of armor Paul talks about is the breastplate of righteousness. Even though we've been made righteous through Christ's blood, we still have to fight a daily battle to strive to be pure. This means we need to guard our hearts. In what ways are

you vulnerable? Considering those things, what steps can you take to guard your heart?

6. Next, Paul talks about feet fitted with "the readiness that comes from the gospel of peace." As you read the three possible applications, which was most challenging to you?

7. In this chapter we also discussed the shield of faith. We are to "dip our shields" daily in the Word by asking God to increase our faith and help us extinguish the fiery darts of the enemy. What are some practical ways you can think of to do that?

8. Just as the breastplate protects the heart, the helmet of salvation protects the mind—the primary site for spiritual warfare. In order to protect our mind, we need to be careful what we ingest by way of our ears, nose, and eyes. Take a moment to think about the things you surround yourself with—music, TV, entertainment, etc. Are there things in your life you should be protecting your mind from?

9. In order to be armed with the sword of the Spirit, we need to have an active plan for reading, studying, meditating, and applying the Bible in our daily experiences. Do you have an active plan? If so, what is it? If not, set aside some time to come up with one.

10. We should constantly be praying—it may well be the most important thing we can do. Do you have a prayer list? If not, write down a list of the people you want to pray for daily, then begin.

How to Use This Book in Small Groups

Agenda

Getting Acquainted

You only get one chance to start. So, having everyone there to meet everyone else, learn names, and connect on a "level playing field" is crucial. DO NOT be so structured in following this conversation guide you keep the Holy Spirit from moving in your group. This is intended to show you one way to navigate your time together.

Conversation Guide

The most important thing you're going to do as you start your group is LISTEN! The leader who is doing all the talking is not a great small group leader!

1. What happened last week you are thankful for?
   - Everyone needs to answer briefly.
2. What challenge is happening in your life, family, or community?
   - Everyone needs to answer briefly.
3. Ask for a volunteer to pray for each person by name.
   - Pray for everyone by name.
   - Thank God for all the blessings on our lives.
   - Pray for the challenges we are facing.
4. Ask if everyone was able to read the assigned chapter.
5. Ask everyone to share one main takeaway from the chapter.
6. Work through the discussion questions in the back of the chapter.
7. Once everyone has had a chance to answer the questions at the end of the chapter, follow these steps:
   - Ask "From what you have read this week and what we discussed today/tonight, what is your 'I will' statement? How are you going to apply this lesson/truth?"
   - Assign the next reading assignment/chapter for the group and confirm date and time of next meeting.
   - Ask "Does anyone feel led to close in prayer?" If no one volunteers, the group leader will voice a short prayer and close out the group.[20]

Outline and Tips

Books

The first order of business is your BOOK ORDER! Be sure to order your books one month in advance from your first group meeting! It is critical that everyone leave your group on Launch Night with the book in hand.

When you realize the average American reads 2.4 books per year, you begin to grasp the potential impact reading one solid, Christian book can have on a person. Reading books in a high accountability context is more like graduate school than reading in a recliner. Knowing you're going to be held accountable for learning the key takeaways and having a conversation with your group about the book will make the learning experience rich. The best group leaders share from their own well of knowledge and experience, so using a book that really speaks to you is best.

Calendar

One of the most "mission critical" activities you'll do at your first session will be setting the calendar for the season. You and your group will need to decide how often you will meet as a group (weekly or bi-weekly) and how long you will meet. Set targets for when you will begin and end. This will prevent the meeting from taking too long. Sixty to ninety minutes is ideal.

Location & Group Size

Keep the groups small. Five is the ideal number, but four to six is okay. Divide larger groups into subgroups and have them work through the questions simultaneously. Plan in advance the location and environment for your group. Make sure you'll have a comfortable place for everyone. Whether around a dining room table, in a den, or in another location, be sure your location is conducive to conversation and prayer. All this will help draw the quiet or shy people into the discussion.

Friendship & Transparency

Another important thing is friendship. You're going to need to be a FRIEND to your group members, invest in them by loving them unconditionally—this means loving them where they are, showing them you're their friend, and listening to them intently. TRANSPARENCY is another important part of being a group leader. This book you will read together is important, and the prayer time is critical, but the real impact of a mature group leader is in sharing his life experiences, both good and bad. That is invaluable.

Pray

Praying for your group, and leading your group to pray for each other, is huge. Be intentional about this, orienting your group to God, encouraging your group to pray for each other and for you between sessions.

Adapted from Final Command Ministries Discovery Group Questions. Used by permission.

ENDNOTES

1   "Captain John Smith," *Colonial Williamsburg Journal* 16, no. 3 (Spring 1994): 14, https://www.history.org/foundation/journal/smith.cfm.

2   Martin Luther, "To the Christian Nobility of the German Nation," *Luther's Works*, ed. Jaroslav Pelikan, (Philadelphia: Fortress Press, 1957), 44:207.

3   Hawkins, John, "5 Reasons Americans Are Living through a Sex Recession," PJ Media, November 19, 2018, https://pjmedia.com/lifestyle/5-reasons-americans-are-living-through-a-sex-recession/.

4   "Blaming Masculinity Will Only Make the Male Crisis Worse," *The Federalist*, January 14, 2019, https://thefederalist.com/2019/01/14/blaming-masculinity-will-make-male-crisis-worse/.

5   William Kilpatrick, "Christianity's Masculinity Crisis," *Crisis Magazine*, February 9, 2019, https://www.crisismagazine.com/2019/christianitys-masculinity-crisis.

6   Thomas Jefferson, "A Summary View of the Rights of British America," *The Papers of Thomas Jefferson*, ed. Julian P. Boyd, Charles T. Cullen, John Catanzariti, and Barbara B. Oberg, (Princeton: Princeton University Press, 1950), 1:135; Thomas Jefferson, "Notes on the State of Virginia, Query XVIII: Manners," *The Writings of Thomas Jefferson*, ed. Paul Leicester Ford, (New York: G. P. Putnam and Sons, 1892–99), 3:267.

7   Mark Beliles and Jerry Newcombe, *Doubting Thomas?: The Religious Life and Legacy of Thomas Jefferson* (New York: Morgan James Publishing, 2015), 378. Jefferson's non-Trinitarian/Unitarian beliefs are first expressed in 1788. See page 378, but also read the entire set of conclusions presented on pages 375–389. The authors fail to give a definite answer to the question "Was Thomas Jefferson a Christian?"

8   Ronald Reagan, *Public Papers of the Presidents of the United States*, (Washington, D.C.: Government Printing Office, 1988), 1374.

9   Jared Sparks, ed., "Proclamation for a National Thanksgiving," *The Writings of George Washington; Being His Correspondence, Addresses, Messages, and Other Papers, Official and Private, Selected and Published from the Original Manuscripts*, (Boston: American Stationer's Company, 1837), 12:119.

10   Charles Francis Adams, ed., letter from John Adams to Thomas Jefferson, 28 June 1813, *The Works of John*

Adams, Second President of the United States, (Boston: Little, Brown and Company, 1856), 10:54.

11   "Proclamation for a Day of Public Thanksgiving," *Columbian Centinel*, vol. 10, October 5, 1791.

12   Roy P. Basler, ed., letter from President Lincoln to A. G. Hodges, Esq., April 4, 1864, *The Collected Works of Abraham Lincoln*, (New Brunswick: Rutgers University Press 1953), 7:281–82.

13   Oshman, Jen, "The Oshman Odyssey," *The Oshman Odyssey* (blog), July 25, 2017, https://www.oshmanodyssey. com/jensblog/n6pb5opplj5kaq12ihl4gahklx7oc1.

14   Dobson, James, "To Protect and Defend," http://drjamesdobson.org/news/ commentaries/to-protect-and-defend.

15   "Bystander Effect," Psychology Today, Sussex Publishers, https://www.psychologytoday.com/us/basics/bystander-effect.

16   Millett, Mallory, "Marxist Feminism's Ruined Lives," *FrontPage Magazine*, September 1, 2014, https://www.frontpagemag.com/fpm/240037/ marxist-feminisms-ruined-lives-mallory-millett.

17   Russell, Nicole, "Disgusting: New York Not Only Legalized Late-Term Abortions, but Also Celebrated like It Won the Super Bowl," *Washington Examiner*, January 23, 2019, https://www.washingtonexaminer.com/opinion/ disgusting-new-york-not-only-legalized-late-term-abortions- but-also-celebrated-like-it-won-the-super-bowl.

[18] "Why Is Friendship Hard for Men? Five Ways to Build Stronger Relationships," Desiring God, December 9, 2018, https://www.desiringgod.org/articles/why-is-friendship-hard-for-men.

[19] Sparks, "Religious Opinions," 401.

[20] These questions were chosen from Discovery Group questions which are being used globally to help catalyze Disciple Making Movements. We acknowledge this is a very different setting than the one for which they were created. Used with permission of Final Command Ministries (www.finalcommand.com).

ABOUT THE AUTHOR

photo © Ron Walters

LTG (R) William G. Boykin is founder of Kingdom Warriors ministry and Executive VP of FRC. He was a founding member and former commander of Delta Force, serving thirty-six years in the US Army. He and his wife Ashley have five children and live in Virginia.

Transcendal Caste

Atmospheric Monitoring with Arduino

Patrick Di Justo and Emily Gertz

O'REILLY®

Beijing · Cambridge · Farnham · Köln · Sebastopol · Tokyo

Atmospheric Monitoring with Arduino
by Patrick Di Justo and Emily Gertz

Published by O'Reilly Media, Inc., 1005 Gravenstein Highway North, Sebastopol, CA 95472.

O'Reilly books may be purchased for educational, business, or sales promotional use. Online editions are also available for most titles (*http://my.safaribooksonline.com*). For more information, contact our corporate/institutional sales department: 800-998-9938 or *corporate@oreilly.com*.

Editors: Shawn Wallace and Brian Jepson
Production Editor: Kara Ebrahim
Proofreader: Kara Ebrahim
Cover Designer: Mark Paglietti
Interior Designer: David Futato
Illustrator: Rebecca Demarest

November 2012: First Edition
December 2012: First Edition

Revision History for the First Edition:

2012-11-19   First release

2012-12-10   Second release

See *http://oreilly.com/catalog/errata.csp?isbn=9781449338145* for release details.

ISBN: 978-1-449-33814-5

[LSI]

We dedicate this book to our sisters and brothers:
Andy, Lucy, Mathius, and Melissa

Contents

Preface

There's a story (it's either an old vaudeville joke or a Zen koan) in which a fisherman asks a fish, "What's the water like down there?" and the fish replies "What is water?" If the story is just a joke, the point is to make us laugh; but if it's a koan, the point is that the most obvious and ubiquitous parts of our immediate environment are, paradoxically, often the easiest to overlook.

We as a species are probably a little bit smarter than fish: at least we know that we spend our lives "swimming" at the bottom of an ocean of air. About 4/5th of that ocean is the relatively harmless gas nitrogen. Around another 1/5 of it is the highly reactive and slightly toxic gas oxygen. The Earth's atmosphere also contains trace amounts of other harmless or slightly toxic gases like argon, carbon dioxide, and methane. And depending on where you live, it may contain even smaller, but much more toxic, amounts of pollutants like soot, carbon monoxide, and ozone.

Yet how many of us, like the fish in the koan, overlook the atmosphere? Who in your life can tell you the general composition of the air around them? How many people know what's inside every breath they take? Do you? Reading this book and building these gadgets will take you on the first steps of a journey toward understanding our ocean of air.

Conventions Used in This Book

The following typographical conventions are used in this book:

Italic

Indicates new terms, URLs, email addresses, filenames, and file extensions.

Constant width
> Used for program listings, as well as within paragraphs to refer to program elements such as variable or function names, databases, data types, environment variables, statements, and keywords.

Constant width bold
> Shows commands or other text that should be typed literally by the user.

Constant width italic
> Shows text that should be replaced with user-supplied values or by values determined by context.

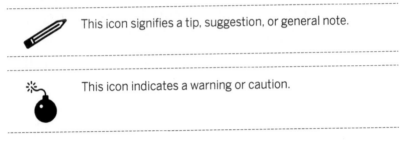

This icon signifies a tip, suggestion, or general note.

This icon indicates a warning or caution.

Using Code Examples

This book is here to help you get your job done. In general, if this book includes code examples, you may use the code in this book in your programs and documentation. You do not need to contact us for permission unless you're reproducing a significant portion of the code. For example, writing a program that uses several chunks of code from this book does not require permission. Selling or distributing a CD-ROM of examples from O'Reilly books does require permission. Answering a question by citing this book and quoting example code does not require permission. Incorporating a significant amount of example code from this book into your product's documentation does require permission.

We appreciate, but do not require, attribution. An attribution usually includes the title, author, publisher, and ISBN. For example: "*Atmospheric Monitoring with Arduino* by Patrick Di Justo and Emily Gertz (O'Reilly). Copyright 2013 Patrick Di Justo and Emily Gertz, 978-1-4493-3814-5."

If you feel your use of code examples falls outside fair use or the permission given above, feel free to contact us at *permissions@oreilly.com*.

Safari® Books Online

Safari Books Online is an on-demand digital library that delivers expert content in both book and video form from the world's leading authors in technology and business.

Technology professionals, software developers, web designers, and business and creative professionals use Safari Books Online as their primary resource for research, problem solving, learning, and certification training.

Safari Books Online offers a range of product mixes and pricing programs for organizations, government agencies, and individuals. Subscribers have access to thousands of books, training videos, and prepublication manuscripts in one fully searchable database from publishers like O'Reilly Media, Prentice Hall Professional, Addison-Wesley Professional, Microsoft Press, Sams, Que, Peachpit Press, Focal Press, Cisco Press, John Wiley & Sons, Syngress, Morgan Kaufmann, IBM Redbooks, Packt, Adobe Press, FT Press, Apress, Manning, New Riders, McGraw-Hill, Jones & Bartlett, Course Technology, and dozens more. For more information about Safari Books Online, please visit us online.

How to Contact Us

You can write to us at:

Maker Media, Inc.
1005 Gravenstein Highway North
Sebastopol, CA 95472
800-998-9938 (in the United States or Canada)
707-829-0515 (international or local)
707-829-0104 (fax)

Maker Media is a division of O'Reilly Media devoted entirely to the growing community of resourceful people who believe that if you can imagine it, you can make it. Consisting of Make magazine, Craft magazine, Maker Faire, as well as the Hacks, Make:Projects, and DIY Science book series, Maker Media encourages the Do-It-Yourself mentality by providing creative inspiration and instruction.

For more information about Maker Media, visit us online:

MAKE: *www.makezine.com*
CRAFT: *www.craftzine.com*
Maker Faire: *www.makerfaire.com*
Hacks: *www.hackszine.com*

We have a web page for this book, where we list examples, errata, examples, and plans for future editions. You can find this page at *http://oreil.ly/atmospheric-arduino*.

To comment or ask technical questions about this book, send email to *book questions@oreilly.com*.

For more information about our books, courses, conferences, and news, see our website at *http://www.oreilly.com*.

Find us on Facebook: *http://facebook.com/oreilly*

Follow us on Twitter: *http://twitter.com/oreillymedia*

Watch us on YouTube: *http://www.youtube.com/oreillymedia*

1/The World's Shortest Electronics Primer

If you're a DIY electronics or Arduino novice, the information in this chapter will help you get the most out of building and programming the gadgets in this book.

If you're already building your own electronics, consider this chapter a refresher to dip into as needed.

What Is Arduino?

Arduino is best described as a single-board computer that is deliberately designed to be used by people who are not experts in electronics, engineering, or programming. It is inexpensive, cross-platform (the Arduino software runs on Windows, Mac OS X, and Linux), and easy to program. Both Arduino hardware and software are open source and extensible.

Arduino is also powerful: despite its compact size, it has about as much computing muscle as one of the original navigation computers from the Apollo program, at about 1/35,000 the price.

Programmers, designers, do-it-yourselfers, and artists around the world take advantage of Arduino's power and simplicity to create all sorts of innovative devices, including interactive sensors, artwork, and toys.

We built each of the products in this book using the Arduino Uno (Figure 1-1 and Figure 1-2), which, at the time of writing, is the latest model. By the time you're reading this, there may be something newer.

You don't have to know Arduino Uno's technical specifications to build and program the gadgets in this book, but if you're interested, you can find them at the official Arduino website (*http://arduino.cc/en/Main/ArduinoBoardUno*).

Figure 1-1. *Front of the Arduino Uno (Rev. 3).*

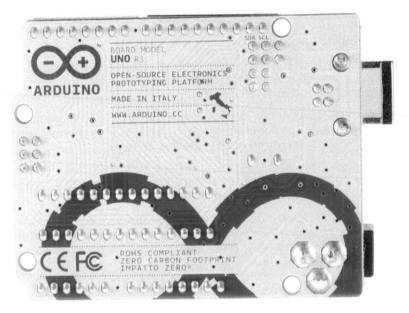

Figure 1-2. *Back of the Arduino Uno.*

Electronic Circuits and Components

An electronic circuit is, as the term implies, electricity moving in a path very much like a circle. Each circuit has a beginning, a middle, and an end (which is usually very close to where it began). Somewhere in the middle, the circuit often runs through various electronic components that modify the electrical current in some way.

Each device in this book is a circuit that combines Arduino with different electronic components. Some of these manage the power and path of the electricity, others sense certain conditions in the environment, and still others display output about those conditions.

Let's take a look at some of the components we will be using in our circuits:

Light emitting diodes (LEDs)

An LED is a lamp made of various rare-earth metals, which give off a large amount of light when a tiny current is run through them. The composition of the substances within the LED determine the particular wavelength of light emitted: you can buy green, blue, yellow, red, even ultraviolet and infrared LEDs.

Technically, the LEDs used in our gadgets are "miniature LEDs," tiny lamps with two wire leads: one long (called the anode) and the other a bit shorter (called the cathode). These come in various useful forms (including single lamps from 2 mm to 8 mm in diameter, display bars, and alphanumeric readouts) and can serve as indicators, illuminators, or even data transmitters.

You'll learn how to use these different types of LEDs while building the different environmental sensors in this book.

Resistors

Resistors are the workhorses of the electronics world. What do resistors do? They simply resist letting electricity flow through by being made of materials that naturally conduct electricity poorly. In this way, resistors serve as small dumb regulators to cut down the intensity of electric current.

Resistance is valuable because some electronic components are very delicate: they burn out easily if they're powered with too much current. Putting a resistor in the circuit ensures that only the proper amount of electricity reaches the component. It's hard to imagine any circuit working without a resistor, and with LEDs, resistors are almost mandatory.

While building the projects in this book, you'll learn various creative ways to regulate current with resistors.

Soldering

Soldering involves heating up conductive metal, called *solder*, and then using it to fuse other pieces of metal together. In small-scale electronics, we use an electrical tool called a soldering iron, which has a small tip, to heat up thin wires of solder and drip the solder onto the components we wish to join into the circuit.

Soldering creates a very stable circuit, and that stability can be a drawback. Fusing together components can make it difficult to reuse or reconfigure circuits. You also must be very careful to not short-circuit components while soldering. Knowing how to solder can be a very useful skill in DIY electronics. If you're interested in learning how, this online resource (*http://mightyohm.com/files/soldercomic/FullSolderComic_20110409.pdf*) is a good place to start.

The alternative to soldering is to use a solderless breadboard.

Solderless breadboards

Solderless breadboards are small plastic boards studded with pins that can hold wires (more about these next). These wires can then be connected to other electronic components, including Arduino.

Solderless breadboards make it much easier to design circuits, because they allow you to quickly try out various assemblies and components without having to solder the pieces together. While solderless breadboards typically are intended for use only in the design phase, many hobbyists keep a breadboard in the final version of a device because they're so fast and easy to use.

If you don't feel like soldering circuit boards, solderless breadboards are the way to go. Each gadget in this book uses a solderless breadboard.

Wire

Wire is the most basic electronic component, creating the path along which electrons move through a circuit. The projects in this book use 1 mm "jumper wires," which have solid metal tips perfectly sized to fit into Arduino and breadboard pins, and come sheathed in various colors of insulation.

 Get as much jumper wire as you can afford, in several colors. When building circuits with Arduino, you can't have too many jumper wires.

We order most of our electronics components from these online retailers:

- Adafruit Industries (*http://adafruit.com*)
- Eemartee (*http://www.emartee.com*)
- Electronic Goldmine (*http://www.goldmine-elec.com*)
- SparkFun (*http://www.sparkfun.com*)

Maker Shed, from MAKE and O'Reilly Media, sells books, kits, and tools, as well as many of the components needed to build the projects in this book including Arduino, breadboards, sensors, and basic electronic components. Maker Shed also supplies convenient bundles for many of the projects in this book (you can find more information about these bundles in the individual project chapters).

Don't count out your friendly local RadioShack (*http://www.radio shack.com*), though. While writing this book, more than once we ran out to RadioShack for a last-minute component.

For years RadioShack cut back on its electronic components inventory, apparently seeing a better future for the business by featuring cell phones and other consumer electronics. But the company has recently begun to embrace the maker movement; at the time of writing, most of their stores around the country are even carrying Arduinos. We're hopeful RadioShack is on the return path to being the hacker heaven it was years ago.

Programming Arduino

A computer program is a coded series of instructions that tells the computer what to do. The programs that run on Arduino are called *sketches*.

The sketches used in this book mostly tell Arduino to read data from one of the pins, such as the one connected to a sensor, and to write information to a different pin, such as the pin connected to an LED or display unit.

Sometimes the sketches also instruct Arduino to process that information in a certain way: to combine data streams, or compare the input with some reference, or even place the data into a readable format.

An Arduino program has two parts: setup() and loop().

setup()
> The setup() part tells Arduino what it needs to know in order to do what we want it to do. For example, setup() tells Arduino which pins it needs to configure as input, which pins to configure as output, and which pins won't be doing much of anything. If we're going to use a special type of output to show our results, such as an LCD display, setup() is where we

tell Arduino how that output works. If we need to communicate with the outside world through a serial port or an ethernet connection, setup() is where we put all the instructions necessary to make that connection work.

loop()

loop() tells Arduino what to do with the input or output. Arduino runs the instructions in loop(), then goes back to the top of loop() and runs them again. And again. And again. loop() continues to loop as long as the Arduino has power.

First Sketch: Make an LED Blink

By long tradition (going back to 2006), the first Arduino sketch you will write is to make an LED blink.

Arduino pins can be used for input and output, as long as you tell the computer which is which. So in this sketch, we tell the Arduino to set pin 13 to be the LED OUTPUT pin, and then we alternately send electricity to pin 13 (setting the pin HIGH) and cut off the electricity to pin 13 (setting the pin LOW). With each alternation, the LED turns on and off.

We'll write all the sketches in this book using the Arduino *integrated development environment* (IDE), which, simply put, is special software for writing and uploading code to Arduino.

Parts

1. Arduino Uno
2. Breadboard
3. LED

Install the IDE

Download the Arduino IDE (*http://arduino.cc/en/Main/Software*), and follow the provided instructions to install it on your computer.

Once you've installed the software, open the IDE. You should see a screen that looks something like Figure 1-3.

Breadboard the Circuit

The circuit portion of this project is very simple: take an LED and place the long lead into pin 13 on Arduino, as you can see in the Figure 1-4 breadboard view.

Figure 1-3. The Arduino IDE on a Mac.

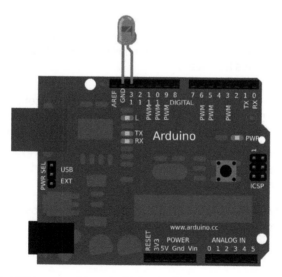

Figure 1-4. LED long lead inserted into pin 13 on the Arduino (image made with Fritzing (http://fritzing.org)).

Write the Code

You can find this code in the Arduino IDE under File → Examples or on the EMWA GitHub Repository → chapter-1 → blink (*https://github.com/ejgertz/EMWA/blob/master/chapter-1/blink*).

```
/*
  Blink
  Turns on an LED for one second,
  then off for one second, repeatedly.
  This example code is based on example code
  that is in the public domain.
*/

void setup() {
  // initialize the digital pin as an output.
  // Pin 13 has an LED connected on most Arduino boards:
  pinMode(13, OUTPUT);
}

void loop() {
  digitalWrite(13, HIGH);    // set the LED on
  delay(1000);               // wait for a second
  digitalWrite(13, LOW);     // set the LED off
  delay(1000);               // wait for a second
}
```

 Normally, you'd need to put a resistor in between the power source and the LED, so as not to burn out the LED. Arduino Unos (and later models) have a resistor built into pin 13, so that's taken care of.

In this sketch, the code in `loop()` simply tells Arduino to set pin 13 HIGH—taking it up to 5 volts—for 1,000 milliseconds (one second), followed by setting it LOW—taking it down to 0 volts—for another 1,000 milliseconds.

Do you notice the /* ... */ sections and the // lines in the example above? Those are ways to put comments into your code to explain to others (and to yourself) what the code does:

- /* and */ tell the computer that everything between those marks should be ignored while running the program.

- // tells the computer that everything afterward on that line is a comment.

Why Comment Code?

Commenting code simply means adding explanations in plain English to your sketch that describe how the code works. Adding comments to code is a very good idea. Here's why:

Suppose, after hours trying to get your Arduino to do something, the solution suddenly comes to you. Eureka! You hook up your Arduino, bang out your code, load it up, and voilà: it works.

Fast forward: months later, working on another project, you want your Arduino to do something similar to your earlier project. "No sweat, I'll just reuse my earlier code," you think. But you open up the sketch and ... none of it makes sense!

You wrote that earlier code in a highly creative state of mind, when your brain chemicals were flowing like a river and your ideas were flashing like summer lightning. In all the excitement, you didn't comment your code. So now, months later, when you're in a completely different state of mind, you can't remember what the code does, and you have to start all over. Is that any way to live?

If you had commented your code from the beginning, you'd know exactly what each variable was used for, what each function did, and what each pin controlled. Your life would be so much more enjoyable.

In short, always take a few minutes to comment your code.

Things to Try

Modify this sketch to make the LED do something different:

1. Blink twice as quickly.
2. Blink twice as slowly.
3. Light up for half a second with a 2-second pause between blinks.

Congratulations, you're an Arduino programmer! Now let's have some real fun.

2/Gadget: Tropospheric Gas Detector

We can easily go several hours without drinking water. We can comfortably go the better part of a day without eating food. But try and go more than a few minutes without breathing. (No, don't really try.) Understanding the composition of the lower atmosphere—the troposphere—is among the most important environmental measurements we can take.

Everything floating around the troposphere—nitrogen, oxygen, carbon dioxide, water vapor, and all sorts of pollution—winds up in our lungs, on our plants, in our food, and in our water (see Figure 2-1). It dusts our windows, our automobiles, and our buildings. For this reason, the authors (as well as organizations like the American Lung Association (*http://www.lung.org/*)) believe that it's vitally important to know what's inside every breath we take.

In the old days, when people wanted to know what was in the atmosphere, they used chemically-treated filter paper, and hung it in a breeze. The chemicals reacted with whatever was in the air and would respond by changing color. Or they bubbled the atmosphere through water and measured the different compounds that resulted as gas dissolved in water. This kind of work could only be performed in a dedicated chemistry lab.

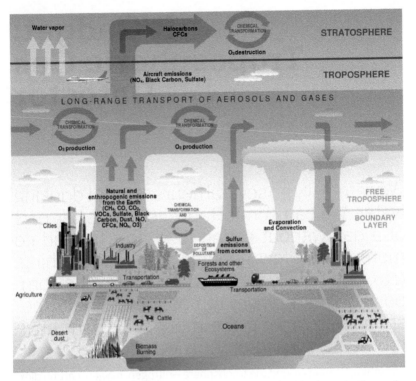

Figure 2-1. *This illustration shows how different chemicals and other substances move into and through the troposphere. Credit: U.S. Climate Change Science Program, 2003.*

Fortunately for us, we can now purchase a small, complete atmospheric laboratory for less than $10, in the form of an electronic gas sensor (Figure 2-2). These sensors detect different substances in the atmosphere by measuring the changing resistance of a film made of tin dioxide.

Figure 2-2. *There are lots of inexpensive sensors on the market that can be used for DIY monitoring.*

How Gas Sensors Work

Oxygen in the atmosphere removes electrons from the tin dioxide film, which decreases its conductivity (and increases its resistance). When other types of gases, particularly those that are chemically reducing, touch the tin dioxide film, electrons are injected into the material. This *increases* the conductivity (and *lowers* the resistance) of the tin dioxide layer. You can use your Arduino to measure that change in resistance.

It's important to keep in mind that tin dioxide sensors tend to be broadly selective. While certain sensors may be marketed as being "alcohol" sensors or "carbon monoxide" sensors, they actually respond to more than just alcohol or carbon monoxide, respectively; they respond to a wide family of similar gases. Manufacturers can make the tin dioxide-based gas sensors more selective by adding various catalysts into the sensor head, or by using external filters. The datasheet provided with each sensor explains more completely how to adjust the sensitivity of each sensor for various gases.

Which Gases Can We Monitor?

There are electronic sensors for a wide range of gases. As we write this book in the summer of 2012, there are easy-to-use inexpensive sensors on the market to detect carbon monoxide, carbon dioxide, liquid petroleum gas, butane, propane, methane (natural gas), hydrogen, ethyl alcohol, benzene, volatile organic compounds, ammonia, ozone, hydrogen sulfide, and more. It's not unreasonable to expect that it won't be long before cheap sensors hit the market that can detect nitrogen oxides and other contaminants. All of these gases count as pollutants; in varying concentrations, all of them can be harmful.

How This Gadget Works

We're going to use the MQ-2 and MQ-6 sensors from Hanwei, Inc. in this gadget. Both detect combustible gases: the MQ-6 detects butane and liquefied petroleum gas (LPG), also called propane (both hydrocarbons), while the MQ-2 is sensitive to LPG, methane (the primary component of natural gas, and a potent greenhouse gas), and smoke. We feel that both sensors together are a great way to start measuring ground-level air pollution.

What Is Smoke?

Smoke, for our purposes, is defined as a byproduct of incompletely burned carbon-based fuel. It includes solid and liquid particulate matter (otherwise known as soot), as well as some gaseous remnants of the original fuel mixed with air. Hanwei's datasheet for the MQ-2 does not specify what "smoke" means for this sensor. But since we know that the MQ-2 detects certain hydrocarbon gases, we're assuming that the smoke it detects is also hydrocarbon-based: a component of automobile or truck exhaust, or the burning of natural gas.

A heating element in the electronic circuit heats the metal, making it more reactive with atmospheric gases. As the various gases react with the metal, the resistance changes in proportion to the amount of that gas present in the air exposed to the sensor. This change in resistance is measured by the Arduino analog port. That's basically it.

If we plug the heater directly into Arduino, we find ourselves with a problem. The heater consumes 800 mW, which works out to equal 200 mA (.8 W / 5

V = .2 A). A standard Arduino pin can only reliably source 20 mA (in other words, only about 10% of the power the heater needs). We have correspondence from the manufacturers indicating that the heater *can* be powered by connecting it to the +5 V Arduino pin, but frankly, we're skeptical. We've got to come up with a way to use Arduino to *control* the amount of power that goes to the heating units, so that the heating unit is not on constantly, without actually having Arduino *provide* that power.

Both these problems—providing power to the heater and controlling that power—have a single solution, probably the greatest invention of the 20th century: the transistor.

Transistorized!

Transistors are used to amplify electronic signals cheaply and efficiently, with very little noise, while giving off very little heat (Figure 2-3). Transistors also act as tiny, efficient digital switches. Since all computer activity breaks down into a series of binary "on and off" states represented by 1s and 0s, transistors by the millions, embedded into a silicon chip, control those on and off signals.

We really can't overstate the importance of the transistor. We don't have room in this book to discuss the details of how transistors work; suffice it to say that the lightweight, cheap electronic gadgets in our lives—handheld cell phones, computers, digital cameras, flat screen TVs, microwave ovens, cable television, touchtone phones, simple portable AM/FM radios, essentially anything more complicated than a flashlight—would be impossible without the transistor.

Figure 2-3. *Various transistors. Source: Ulf Seifert.*

The first thing you notice when you look at a transistor is that unlike almost every other electronic device we've seen so far, a transistor has three terminals. We can control the voltage between two of the terminals by applying a specific electric current or voltage to the third terminal. The three terminals are the base, the collector, and the emitter. The base is the controller; voltage applied here determines whether or not electricity flows from the collector to the emitter. The collector is the "source" of the electrical current, and the emitter is the output.

If we were to send varying levels of current from the base, we can regulate the amount of current flowing from the collector to the emitter. This is how a transistor acts as an amplifier: a very low signal coming into the base is repeated at a much larger voltage provided by the collector.

When we use a transistor as a switch, the circuitry is even simpler. A transistor switch is either fully on or fully off. A small data signal to the base determines whether the transistor is switched on or off. When it is switched on, current flows between the ground and the collector. This simple setup lets us use Arduino to turn on components that have a separate power supply.

Build the Gadget

Amount	Part Type	Properties/(Assembly Code)
2	1 k Ω resistor	Package THT; tolerance 5%; bands 4; resistance 1 k Ω; pin spacing 400 mil (R1 & R2)
1	Voltage regulator, 5 V	Package TO220 [THT]; voltage 5 V (U1)
2	NPN-transistor	Package TO92 [THT]; type NPN (Q1 & Q2)
1	Arduino UNO R3	(Arduino1)
1	LCD screen	Character type, 16 pins (LCD1)
1	Battery block 9 V	(VCC1)

1. Connect a wire from the GND pin of Arduino to the GND rail of the breadboard. Connect the GND rail of the breadboard to the EMITTER pin of the transistor (Figure 2-4).

2. Connect the BASE pin of the transistor to a 1 K resistor, and connect the resistor to an Arduino digital pin (Figure 2-5).

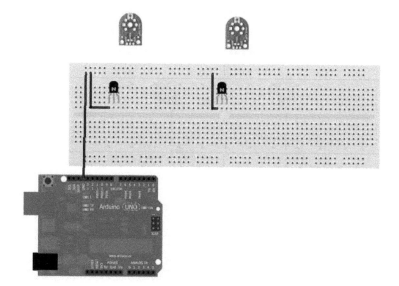

Figure 2-4. *Step one. Source: these images were created with Fritzing (http://fritzing.org).*

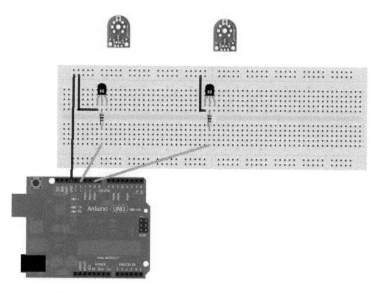

Figure 2-5. *Step two.*

3. Connect the COLLECTOR pin of the transistor to the GND pin of the sensor (Figure 2-6).

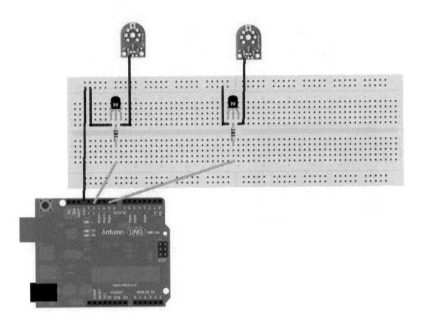

Figure 2-6. *Step three.*

4. Connect the +5 (VCC) sensor pins to the breadboard's power rail (Figure 2-7). Don't worry; we're going to add a power supply later.
5. Connect the data lines from the sensors to Arduino analog ports 4 and 5 (Figure 2-8).

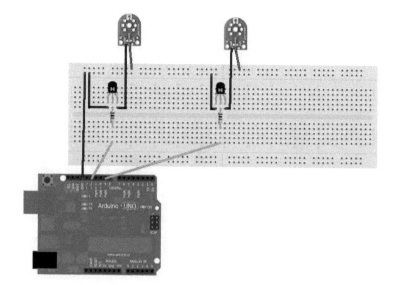

Figure 2-7. *Step four.*

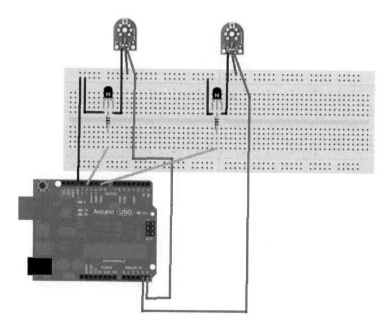

Figure 2-8. *Step five.*

6. Connect the 7805 +5 VDC voltage regulator. This regulates the voltage coming from your independent power source for the sensor heaters. Like the transistor, the voltage regulator also has three terminals: a center pin goes to GND, the pin on the left is input, and the pin on the right is output (Figure 2-9).

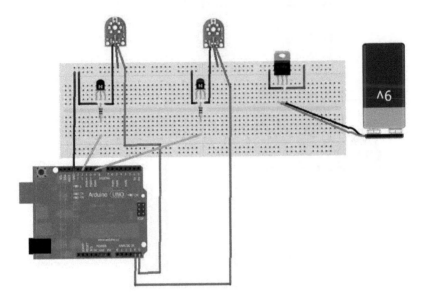

Figure 2-9. *Step six.*

7. Connect the GND pin to the GND rail of the breadboard AND to the black (or −) wire on your power supply. Connect the input pin to the red (or +) wire on your power supply. Connect the output pin to the power rail on the breadboard (Figure 2-10).

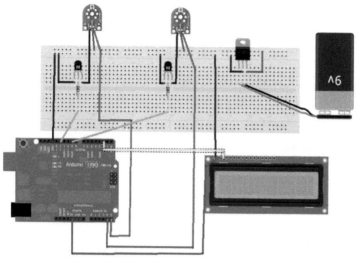

Figure 2-10. *Step seven.*

This device takes an input current (up to 35 volts), and changes it to a stable, fixed +5 VDC. In our example, we're using a standard 9 volt battery at the current source, but you can use just about anything: a 6 volt lantern battery, two 3.7 volt lithium polymer batteries connected in series, even a bunch of AA batteries. The total capacity of your power source should be your main determining factor: smaller batteries generally provide fewer amp-hours, meaning that the lifespan of your gadget can be cut short if you run out of power.

Don't connect the battery until you actually need it, or add an ON-OFF switch to power it up when you're ready to start taking readings.

Optionally, connect the LCD. The data line is Arduino pin 2, ground goes to GND, and the power supply is Arduino's 3.3 V pin.

Load the Sketch

You can find this sketch in the AMWA GitHub repository (*https://github.com/ejgertz/AMWA*).

```
#include <SoftwareSerial.h>
#include <SD.h>
#include <EEPROM.h>
#include<stdlib.h>
```

```
// Liquid Crystal Display
// Define the LCD pins: We'll be using a serial-based LCD display
// which only required +3.3Volts, GND, and a single data line.
// databuff and displaybuff hold the data to be displayed
#define LCDIn 2
#define LCDOut 5
SoftwareSerial mySerialPort(LCDIn, LCDOut);


// Data Buffers for the LCD
char databuff1[16];
char databuff2[16];
char dispbuff[16];

// GAS SENSORS
// Analog input pin that reads the first gas sensor
const int gasPin1 = A5;

// Analog input pin that reads the gas sensor
const int gasPin2 = A4;

// The digital pin that controls the heater of gas sensor 1
const int heaterPin1 = 7;

// The digital pin that controls the heater of gas sensor 2
const int heaterPin2 = 9;

// LED connected to digital pin 13
const int ledPin = 13;

// value read from the sensor A5
int gasVal1 = 0;

// value read from the sensor A4
int gasVal2 = 0;

long warmup = 180000;               // enter time for heaters to warmup, in
milliseconds.
// 180,000 milliseconds = 3 minutes

long downtime = 360000;             // enter delay between readings, in
milliseconds.
// 360,000 milli seconds = 6 minutes

//EEPROM records require two bytes to store a 1024 bit value.
//Each gas sensor returns a value from 0-1024, taking 2 bytes.
//To store gas sensor data would require a record index,
//plus two bytes for the first gas sensor, two bytes for the second gas
sensor
//For a total of five bytes per record.

// current EEPROM address
int addr =0;

//EEPROM record number
```

```
int record = 0;

//EEPROM record length
int reclen = 5;

//switch to tell if an SD card is present
int SDPresent = 1;

void setup()
{
  // initialize serial communications at 9600 bps:
  Serial.begin(9600);

  pinMode(heaterPin1, OUTPUT);  // sets the digital pins as output
  pinMode(heaterPin2, OUTPUT);
  pinMode(LCDOut, OUTPUT);

  //reset the LCD
  mySerialPort.begin(9600);
  mySerialPort.write(0xFE);
  mySerialPort.write(0x01);
  sprintf(databuff1,"Wakeup Test");
  sprintf(dispbuff,"%-16s",databuff1);
  mySerialPort.print(dispbuff);

  // Set up SD card, let us know if SD card is absent
  pinMode(10, OUTPUT);
  if (!SD.begin(4))
  {
    SDPresent =0;
    sprintf(databuff2,"NO SD CARD!!!");
    sprintf(dispbuff,"%-16s",databuff2);
    mySerialPort.print(dispbuff);
    Serial.println("NO SD CARD!!!");
    delay(6000);
  }
  delay(3333);
}

void loop()
{
  long scratch=0;    // scratch variable

  // set the timer
  unsigned long counter = millis();

  //turn first heater on
  digitalWrite(heaterPin1, HIGH);

  // wait 3 minutes for heater to heat up
  while(millis() < (counter + warmup))
  {
    sprintf(databuff1,"Unit1 Activated");
    sprintf(dispbuff,"%-16s",databuff1);
    mySerialPort.print(dispbuff);
```

```
    scratch = (int)((counter+warmup - millis())/1000);
    sprintf(databuff2,"Countdown: %3d", scratch);
    sprintf(dispbuff,"%-16s",databuff2);
    mySerialPort.print(dispbuff);

    Serial.println(scratch);
}

// read the analog in value:
gasVal1 = analogRead(gasPin1);
sprintf(databuff1,"read unit 1");
sprintf(dispbuff,"%-16s",databuff1);
mySerialPort.print(dispbuff);

// shut off the first heater
digitalWrite(heaterPin1, LOW);

//turn second heater on
digitalWrite(heaterPin2, HIGH);
sprintf(databuff2,"turning on unit2");
sprintf(dispbuff,"%-16s",databuff2);
mySerialPort.print(dispbuff);

// wait 3 minutes for heater to heat up
while(millis() < (counter + warmup + warmup))
{
    sprintf(databuff1,"Unit2 Activated");
    sprintf(dispbuff,"%-16s",databuff1);
    mySerialPort.print(dispbuff);

    scratch = (int)((counter+warmup+warmup - millis())/1000);
    sprintf(databuff2,"Countdown: %3d", scratch);
    sprintf(dispbuff,"%-16s",databuff2);
    mySerialPort.print(dispbuff);

    Serial.println(scratch);
}

// read the analog in value:
gasVal2 = analogRead(gasPin2);
sprintf(databuff2,"reading unit2");
sprintf(dispbuff,"%-16s",databuff2);
mySerialPort.print(dispbuff);

// shut off the second heater
digitalWrite(heaterPin2, LOW);

//Display on LCD
sprintf(databuff1,"Gas1:%4d",gasVal1);
sprintf(dispbuff,"%-16s",databuff1);
mySerialPort.print(dispbuff);
sprintf(databuff2,"Gas2:%4d",gasVal2);
sprintf(dispbuff,"%-16s",databuff2);
mySerialPort.print(dispbuff);
```

```
//write to SD card
  if(SDPresent = 1)
  {
    writeDataToSD(databuff1, databuff2);
  }

  //Wait downtime and start again
  //to make more frequent measurements, change value of downtime
  while(millis() < (counter +downtime))
  {
  }
}

void writeDataToSD(String dataString1, String dataString2)
{
  // open the file. note that only one file can be open at a time,
  // so you have to close this one before opening another.
  File dataFile = SD.open("datalog.txt", FILE_WRITE);

  // if the file is available, write to it:
  if (dataFile)
  {
    Serial.println("Hooray, we have a file!");
    dataFile.print(millis());
    dataFile.print(",");
    dataFile.print(dataString1);
    dataFile.print(",");
    dataFile.println(dataString2);

    dataFile.close();

    // print to the serial port too:
    Serial.print(millis());
    Serial.print(",");
    Serial.print(dataString1);
    Serial.print(",");
    Serial.println(dataString2);

    //Print to LCD
    mySerialPort.print("Datafile written");
  }
}
```

Displaying and Storing Your Data

You can connect Arduino to components that display data, as well as those that store data for later use.

Liquid Crystal Displays

Liquid crystal displays (LCDs) are cheap and easy ways to display data, status, warnings, and other messages from Arduino. They come in many different colors: you can buy LCDs with amber characters on a black background, black characters on a green background, yellow characters on a blue background, and other color combinations. Some LCDs have two rows of 16 characters, others four rows of 20 characters, and other display combinations are available as well. But for our uses, the biggest differences in LCDs involve the way they handle data.

The most basic (and least expensive) LCDs make you do all the data handling. They can take up as many as 10 digital data pins (most Arduinos only have 13), and might even require you to design your own characters. Some makers love doing stuff like that, but others just want to plug in a device and have it work.

For our uses, we've decided to go with a serial-controlled LCD, one in which a small microprocessor attached to the LCD takes care of all the data and character management. It's more expensive, but also much easier to use. All we need to do is ground the device, give it some power, and feed it data.

Step seven of the build explains how to connect the LCD to the tropospheric gas detector.

Reading Data Off EEPROM

You might have noticed in the code that Arduino writes the data it recieves to something called EEPROM. This stands for "Electrically Erasable Programmable Read-Only Memory." This is a type of computer memory that is nonvolatile; it remains in place after Arduino is powered down, or after a new program is loaded. EEPROM is perfect for storing data that has to last a long time (a long time by Arduino standards, that is), such as months or years. Our gadget uses 5 bytes of EEPROM to store a single observation record: 1 byte for the record number, and 2 bytes apiece for each sensor's data.

We've included a small program to extract tropospheric gas data from the Arduino's EEPROM. Simply connect your Arduino to your computer via the USB cable, upload the following sketch, and then view the serial monitor.

```
#include <EEPROM.h>

// start reading from the first byte (address 0) of the EEPROM

int address = 1;
int record = 0;
unsigned int Sensor1 = 0;
unsigned int Sensor2 = 0;

int q;
int m;

void setup()
{
  Serial.begin(9600);
```

```
      Serial.println("Record#, Sensor1, Sensor2");
      for(int i =0; i<=95; i++)
      {
        readData();
      }
}

void loop()
{
  // There's no need for this program to loop.  We know what we want to do,
  // and we just did it in setup().
}

void readData()
{
  record = EEPROM.read(address++);
  Serial.print(record);
  Serial.print(",");
  q = EEPROM.read(address++);
  delay(20);
  m = EEPROM.read(address++);
  delay(20);
  Sensor1 = (q*256)+m;

  Serial.print(Sensor1);
  Serial.print(",");
  q = EEPROM.read(address++);
  delay(20);
  m = EEPROM.read(address++);
  delay(20);
  Sensor2 = (q*256)+m;

  Serial.print(Sensor2);
  Serial.print(",");
  q = EEPROM.read(address++);
  delay(20);
  m = EEPROM.read(address++);
  delay(20);

}
```

The result is a CSV display of your data, ready to be copied and pasted into your favorite spreadsheet program.

The Limits of EEPROM

EEPROM is not limitless. The Arduino Duemilanove and Uno each have a single kilobyte of EEPROM available, which (at 5 bytes per observation record) will hold about 200 observations worth of data. At 5 observations per hour, that's enough for more than a day and a half of solid observation. Arduino Megas have 4 kilobytes of EEPROM, about enough to hold a week's worth of atmospheric data. The old Arduino NGs, Nanos, and Diecimilas have a paltry 512 bytes of EEPROM, about 20 hours' worth.

What do you do when your EEPROM is full? The Arduino IDE has a sketch called EEPROM_Clear. Simply run that, and it will wipe your Arduino's non-volatile memory and make it ready for the next season's worth of data. Of course, you will have already backed up your data to a spreadsheet, a hard drive, an SD card, or Cosm before you wipe your EEPROM, right?

Reading Data from an SD Card

If you are storing your gas detector data on the SD card, you'll find a file called *DATALOG.TXT*. That file contains your measurements in CSV (comma separated value) format. To save space on Arduino, we did not massage the data in any way. You can open this file in your favorite spreadsheet program and work with it as desired.

Things to Try

Of course, there's not just one way to build a gas detector. There are many different configurations you can try (such as more or different sensors) that will provide more detailed data, but what changes (if any) will you have to make to the circuit to be sure it works properly? Will you need to beef up the batteries, or try a totally new power source? Here are some other ideas to make your gas detector more versatile.

Other Sensors

Does hot humid air hold more pollution than cold dry air? If you add a temperature/humidity sensor to the gadget, can you detect any correlations between temperature/humidity and toxic gas concentration?

As we noted earlier, Hanwei and other manufacturers offer many different gas sensors, often (but not always) built around the same basic circuitry, making it relatively easy to add more sensors to a gadget, or swap new sensors for old ones. It might be interesting to add an MQ-131 ozone sensor to the MQ-2 and MQ-6 sensors—is there a correlation between automobile pollution and ozone? between temperature/humidity and ozone?

Solar Powered

One drawback to the current gadget is the batteries last only a few days. Is it possible to have the gadget work forever by powering it with the sun?

Yes, with some caveats. The heating elements of the gas sensors are real power hogs, and running this device totally on solar power might or might not be practical depending on the size of the solar panel, the amount of sunlight at your location, and the number of gas sensors you have. If you want to give it a try, we'd recommend starting with something like the Adafruit USB/SOLAR LiPoly charger (*http://ladyada.net/products/usbdcsolarlipo/*). This device will handle all the power management for you.

The key question is the size of the solar panel: if you calculate the amount of power your Arduino and sensors use, and compare it to the net power you can expect from the solar panel/charger (taking into account your location and time of year), you can get a good idea if solar will work for your gadget.

GSM

Wouldn't it be great if, instead of having to fetch data from your gadget, you could make your gadget send you its data? You can, with a GSM module. This device, available from all the usual suppliers like Sparkfun and Adafruit, is essentially the guts of a cell phone without the keypad, display, speaker, microphone, or ringtones. By connecting it in place of (or along with) the LCD display, you can have your gadget send you text messages (or even post on Twitter!) its latest findings. You'll need to get a separate SIM card with a data plan, but these usually cost in the range of $5 to $10 per month.

Do Not Deploy Your Gadget in Public Without Official Permission

Now we come to the strangest part of this book: the warning not to leave your gas detector unattended, anywhere, ever. Here's why:

In May 2012, Takeshi Miyakawa, a visual artist and furniture designer in New York City, placed a portable battery-powered light inside a translucent "I Love NY" plastic shopping bag, and hung it from a metal rod attached to a tree. When the lamp was on, the bag glowed from within. A friend of the artist said he did this "to lift people's spirits. He was simply trying to say that he loves the city and spread that attitude around."

Unfortunately for Miyakawa, someone in the neighborhood saw a contraption with wires, batteries, and plastic boxes and called the New York Police Department's bomb squad, which evacuated the area and took two hours to determine that a battery and a light was just a battery and a light. When the police tracked the device to Miyakawa, they arrested him and charged him with two counts of first-degree reckless endangerment, two counts of placing a false bomb or hazardous substance in the first degree, two counts of placing a false bomb or hazardous substance in the second degree, two counts of second-degree reckless endangerment, and two counts of second-degree criminal nuisance. A judge ordered him sent to Bellevue hospital for psychiatric evaluation, as well.

All for hanging a light in a tree.

Miyakawa's experience is not unique, unfortunately. In another case, researchers from Carnegie-Mellon University built similar detectors to ours, and placed them at various points around the Pittsburgh area. While the sensors were enclosed in professionally made plastic cases, and were clearly labeled as an approved research project, once again the police bomb squad was called. (The students didn't report being arrested. However, they did say it took a great deal of negotiation with the authorities to get their equipment back.)

The US Department of Homeland Security (DHS) urges people to "be vigilant, take notice of your surroundings, and report suspicious items or activities to local authorities immediately." As a result, homemade electronic gadgets that once upon a time (at least, in the lifetimes of the authors) might have been regarded as interesting curiosities are now treated as threats. Many people don't understand hobby electronics, and are frightened by what they do not understand. Police believe they must treat every suspicious package as if it may be harmful.

The point of telling you all this is not to scare you from building monitoring devices, but to warn you that a home-built, Arduino-based gas sensor might, to the unknowing eye, look like a box of batteries and wires and a scary thing with blinking lights. Leaving something like this unattended, without permission, on property you don't own, can get you into a world of trouble.

The following subsections are a couple ideas for solving this problem.

Get Official Permission

Look into official channels through which you can deploy experimental packages in public. At A.M.W.A. World Headquarters in New York City, we looked to the Parks Department, which allows researchers to leave experimental devices in some of the city's parks. The entire application process is on the city's website. It's fairly extensive, requiring an explanation of the experiment and a description of the device, but can be filled out in a single sitting.

Unfortunately, processing these permits seems to take a long time. We applied for one in early May 2012, and it still hadn't arrived by the time this book went to press in November.

Get Your Community Involved

- If you're a student, get your teachers on your side when it comes to your projects. Arduino is so new that there's a good chance you'll be teaching the teachers for a change, and once your teachers understand what you're doing, they'll be among your staunchest supporters.

- If you're a member of a hackerspace, have an open house. Invite members of the community to meet you in person and learn about what you're doing. This may work wonders toward alleviating some of the public's fear of DIY electronics.

- If you're not a member of a hackerspace, consider joining one, or even starting one. Good online resources for finding and learning more about hackerspaces are the Hackerspace Wiki (*http://hackerspaces.org/wiki/*) and the UK Hackspace Foundation (*http://hackspace.org.uk/view/Starting_a_Hackerspace*).

3/A Brief Introduction to LEDs

Before we start working on the LED photometer, we're going to take a brief look at why and how the gadget's crucial component—the light emitting diode, or LED—can be used to monitor certain properties of the atmosphere.

Even if you've worked with LEDs before, chances are your projects used them simply as lights or indicators of some sort, with the color choices more about aesthetics than science. By comparison, in this book we use LEDs in ways that take advantage of the physics of light.

We think you'll get more out of building and using the LED photometer if you know more about that. But if you're feeling impatient, skip to the project in Chapter 4, the LED Sensitivity Tester, and proceed from there.

It is essential to test your LEDs before you build the LED photometer. Testing takes two forms: (1) testing to see if the LEDs light up and (2) testing the LEDs for wavelength sensitivity. The first test is easy: you can connect the short wire of an LED to Arduino GND and the long end to pin 13, and run the BLINK sketch that comes with the Arduino IDE software; if the LED blinks, it works. (An even easier way is to connect an LED to a 3 v coin cell—with the long wire on the positive side of the battery. If the LED lights, it works.)

Testing the LED for wavelength sensitivity is much more complicated; we deal with that in Chapter 4.

What Is a Diode?

A diode is a two-terminal electronic device that lets electricity flow easily in one direction, and prevents (or resists) it from flowing in the other direction.

Many electrical components can be run "backwards": for example, a loud-speaker can be used as a microphone, and vice versa. A motor, which turns electricity into movement, can often be used as a generator that turns movement into electricity.

This reversibility of electronic components is partly thanks to the fact that electricity usually has no problem flowing both ways through a circuit; it makes no difference to an electron if it flows from a battery to a motor or from a motor to a battery.

But the direction of electron flow matters if we're designing a generator circuit: we don't want that circuit to suddenly work in reverse and start spinning like a motor! This is where diodes are useful. They work like valves that prevent the "backflow" of electricity, ensuring that electrons will move only in the direction we want them to.

Discovery of the Diode

The 1870s were an exciting time to be working with electricity. In America, Thomas Edison was inventing some of the devices that would define the 20th century: the light bulb, the phonograph, and an improved telephone. Meanwhile in Europe, scientists were taking a more theoretical approach, seeking to understand how electricity flowed.

In 1874, a German scientist named Karl Ferdinand Braun published an account of what he called "the unilateral conduction of current by natural metal sulfides." Up to this point, scientists knew that electricity could travel along a wire in either direction. Braun discovered that a crystal of tetrahedrite (a compound of copper, antimony, and sulfur) let electricity flow through it in only one direction. This demonstration of one-way electrical flow was the first known semiconductor diode—in fact, it was the first semiconductor in history.

What Is a Light Emitting Diode?

A light emitting diode is a diode that emits light.

Okay, snark aside, in 1907 a scientist named Henry Joseph Round discovered that crystals of carborundum gave off a faint yellow light when they were energized by electrons. These crystals were also diodes, and didn't emit light when electricity tried to flow the other way. Scientists later discovered that in an LED, electrons combine with electron "holes" in the crystal, and release excess energy as photons in a very narrow range of wavelengths known as the emission band. The narrowness of this emission band is rivaled only by laser light, and explains the jewel-like purity of LED light.

Figure 3-1 shows some LEDs in sizes 8 mm, 5 mm, and 3 mm. Two important things to know for DIY purposes are that the longer lead is called the anode (commonly thought of as the positive terminal), and the shorter lead is called the cathode (commonly thought of as the negative terminal). An easy way to remember this is that the negative terminal has something "subtracted" from it. Because an LED is a diode, electricity will only easily flow through it in one direction. So when you plug an LED into a circuit, be sure to connect the anode to the positive side of the circuit and the cathode to the negative side or ground, if you expect to make it glow.

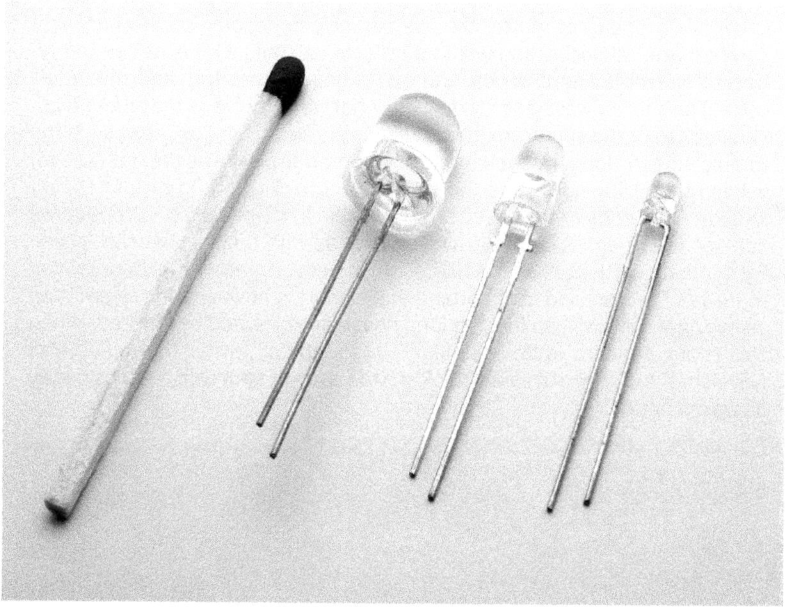

Figure 3-1. *LEDs in 8 mm, 5 mm, and 3 mm sizes.*

How Are We Using LEDs in the LED Photometer?

LEDs not only emit light; they absorb it, too. An amateur scientist discovered this capability of LEDs in the 1970s. Forrest M. Mims III, a former US Air Force officer, had been doing experiments with photocells and light since he was a boy. Understanding that many electronic devices can be run "backwards" [see "What Is a Diode?" (page 33)], Mims reasoned that since LEDs take in electricity and emit light (along that narrow emission band, remember), they should also take in light and give off electricity. A series of experiments proved him right, and by 1973 he had formalized what is now known as the Mims Effect: LEDs will absorb light along a relatively narrow band of color, and emit a small amount of electricity. These light-absorbing qualities of LEDs are what we put to work in our LED photometer.

An LED absorbs light occurring in wavelengths near its own emission band, or slightly shorter. A green LED absorbs light in the greenish-blue part of the spectrum, a red LED absorbs light in the reddish-orange part of the spectrum, and so on. We can use this difference in the way LEDs absorb light to tell us a great deal about the atmosphere.

What Is Color?

Color is a property of matter that we perceive depending upon which light waves matter absorbs, and which it reflects or emits. Our eyes see the reflected or emitted light waves, and our brains process that information as color. The shorter wavelengths occur in what we percieve as the blue-indigo-violet range of the spectrum; the wavelengths we think of as green sit in the middle; and the longer wavelengths occur in what we see as the red-orange-yellow range. Ultraviolet (a very short wavelength of light) and infrared (a very long one) are ends of the spectrum not visible to human eyes—although we can see the re-emission of ultraviolet light, as with the psychedelic "black-light" posters of the 1960s and 1970s, which were printed with inks containing materials that excelled at absorbing those short light waves and re-emitting visible light. And we can feel the long heat waves created by infrared. When something appears white in sunlight, it is made of matter that reflects all wavelengths of light; if it looks black, it's made up of stuff that absorbs nearly all wavelengths.

4/Gadget: LED Sensitivity Tester

Before building and using the LED photometer, we first need to figure out exactly which wavelengths of light each of our LEDs is sensitive to. Otherwise, we won't be able to get good data with the photometer. Unfortunately, no LED datasheet that we've ever seen troubles itself with listing LED input wavelength, because LED manufacturers generally don't think of their products as input devices. Fortunately, we can determine input wavelengths with a gadget we can build ourselves: the LED sensitivity detector.

Mission: Inputtable

Your mission, should you choose to accept it, is to determine the peak input wavelength for a series of LEDs. You will do this by shining every wavelength of visible light, from 350–700 nm, into each candidate LED, and measuring that LED's responsive voltage. The LED that's most sensitive to the wavelength is the one that produces the highest response voltage. Good luck.

How are we going to generate every visible wavelength of light to test our LEDs, from ultraviolet to infrared? If your answer is "use a full-spectrum LED," you're correct. This special type of LED is called an RGB LED and it can output red light, green light, blue light, and any combination of those colors: the full ROY G. BIV. Since it's beyond the scope of this book to go too deeply into the science of combining light to make different colors, suffice it to say that by mixing varying intensities of red, green, and blue light, just about any color can be reproduced. (Look very carefully at the pixels of your computer screen to see this in action.)

Amount	Part Type	Properties/(Assembly Code)
1	Loudspeaker	(SPKR1)
1	TEST LED, 5 mm	5 mm [THT]; (LED2)
1	RGB LED (com. anode, rbg)	5 mm [THT]; pin order rgb; polarity common anode; rgb RGB (LED1)
2	47 Ω resistor	Package THT; tolerance ffl5%; bands 4; resistance 47 Ω; pin spacing 400 mil (R1 & R2)
1	62 Ω resistor	Package THT; tolerance ffl5%; bands 4; resistance 62 Ω; pin spacing 400 mil (R3)
1	Arduino UNO R3	(Arduino1)
1	LCD screen	Character type 16 pins (LCD1)
1	Permanent marker in a dark color	

Build the Gadget

1. **Connect the RGB LED to Arduino.** Most RGB LEDs are common anode, so follow the datasheet that came with your LED to connect the anode to the +5 pin on Arduino (Figure 4-1). The R, G, and B pins should be connected to Arduino pins 8, 6, and 4, respectively. For our RGB LED, the red cathode needed a 62 ohm resistor, while the green and blue cathodes needed a 47 ohm resistor. (Your values may vary.)

 When we say "connect an LED to Arduino" in these instructions, we intend for you to do this via a breadboard and jumper wires, as illustrated in the figures for each step. Given the amount of gadget handling involved in testing a bunch of LEDs, using a breadboard will save a lot of wear and tear on Arduino.

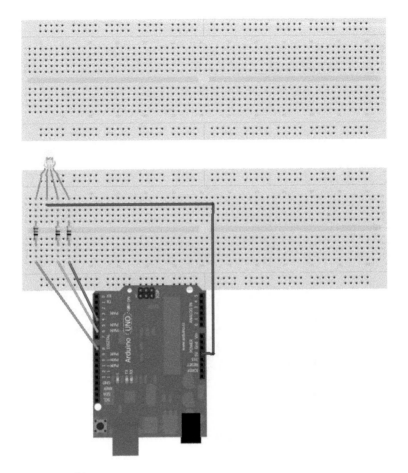

Figure 4-1. *Step one.*

2. **Connect the LCD.** Connect the common ground lead on the LCD (screen display) to the GND pin on Arduino. Connect the VCC lead on the LCD to the 3.3 power pin on Arduino. Connect the DATA lead on the LCD to Arduino pin 2 (Figure 4-2).

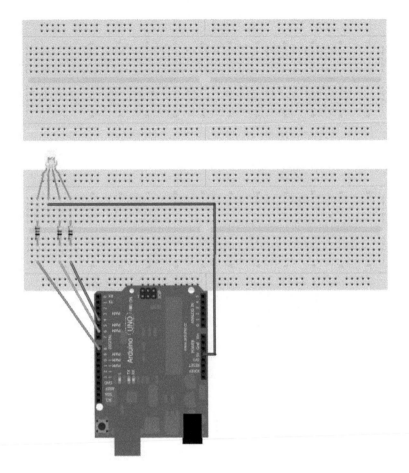

Figure 4-2. *Step two.*

3. **Add an audio speaker for additional fun.** Connect the speaker's black wire to GND on Arduino, and the speaker's red wire to Arduino pin 8. The schematic looks something like Figure 4-3.

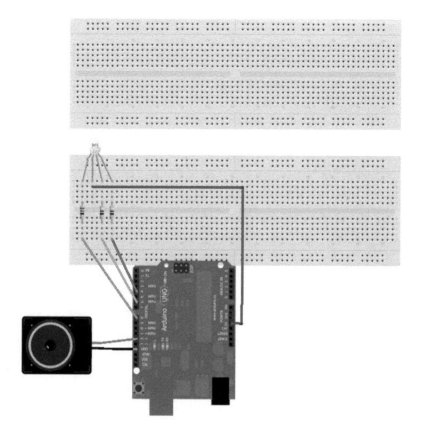

Figure 4-3. *Step three.*

4. **Load the sketch.** Now we need a way to translate a wavelength of light into its red, green, and blue values. Fortunately, a scientist named Dan Brunton has developed a formula that will do just that. We programmed Brunton's algorithm into the following Arduino sketch. After setting up all the components, running this code will cause the RGB LED to emit light from 350–700 nm, the range of visible light.

You can find this sketch in the AMWA GitHub repository (*https://github.com/ejgertz/AMWA*).

```
/**
 * Determining RGB color from a wavelength
 * The code is based on an algorithm from Dan Bruton's Color Science Page.
 * http://www.midnightkite.com/color.html
 * by Patrick Di Justo
 * 2012 08 28
 *
```

```
**/

#include <EEPROM.h>
#include <SoftwareSerial.h>

//Set up the Liquid Crystal Display
#define LCDIn 3
#define LCDOut 2
SoftwareSerial mySerialPort(LCDIn, LCDOut);

//LCD Display buffers
char databuff[16];
char dispbuff[16];

// Variables needed for RGB calculations
float Gamma = 1.00;
int MaxIntensity = 255;
float fBlue;
float fGreen;
float fRed;
float Factor;

int iR;
int iG;
int iB;

//Our eyes can generally see light wavelengths between 350 and 700
nanometers.
//Here, we start the RGB Led with 350
int i = 350;

//RGB is plugged into these arduino digital pins
const int redOutPin = 8;
const int greenOutPin = 6;
const int blueOutPin = 4;

// LED to be tested is plugged into A0
int testPin = A0;

// variables to store the value coming from the sensor
int sensorValueTest =0;
int oldTest =0;
int peaknm =0;

//EEPROM start data
int addr=0;

//Music
int notelen = 90;
int dlx = 130;

void setup()
{
  pinMode(LCDOut, OUTPUT);
  pinMode(LCDIn, INPUT);
```

```
//Set the RGB LED pins to output

  pinMode(redOutPin, OUTPUT);
  pinMode(greenOutPin, OUTPUT);
  pinMode(blueOutPin, OUTPUT);


// Initialize the LCD display
  mySerialPort.begin(9600);
  mySerialPort.write(0xFE);
  mySerialPort.write(0x01);

  // test to see if the RGB LED works
  makeColor(i);
  analogWrite(redOutPin,255-iR);
  analogWrite(greenOutPin, 255-iG);
  analogWrite(blueOutPin, 255-iB);
  delay(5000);
}

void loop()
{

// set the RGB LED to a specific color
  makeColor(i);
  analogWrite(redOutPin, 255-iR);
  analogWrite(greenOutPin, 255-iG);
  analogWrite(blueOutPin, 255-iB);
  delay(500);

// read the sensitivity of the Test LED
  sensorValueTest= analogRead(testPin);

  if (sensorValueTest > oldTest)
  {
    oldTest = sensorValueTest;
    peaknm = i;
  }

// Display the values on the LCD
  sprintf(databuff,"CV:%3d Cnm:%3d",sensorValueTest,i);
  sprintf(dispbuff,"%-16s",databuff);
  mySerialPort.print(dispbuff);

  sprintf(databuff,"XV:%3d Xnm:%3d",oldTest, peaknm);
  sprintf(dispbuff,"%-16s",databuff);
  mySerialPort.print(dispbuff);


  writeData();
  i++;

  // If we've reached the upper limit of 700 nm, play a little melody
```

```
    if (i>700)
    {
      for (int f = 0; f<=100; f++)
      {
        tone(7,196,notelen);
        delay(dlx);

        tone(7,131,notelen);
        delay(dlx);

        tone(7,261,notelen);
        delay(dlx);

        tone(7,330,notelen);
        delay(dlx);

        tone(7,294,notelen);
      }
      delay(10000);
    }
}


void writeData()
{
  int quotient = i/256;
  int mod = i % 256;

  EEPROM.write(addr++,quotient);
  EEPROM.write(addr++,mod);

  quotient = sensorValueTest/256;
  mod = sensorValueTest % 256;
  EEPROM.write(addr++,quotient);
  EEPROM.write(addr++,mod);
}


void makeColor(int lambda)
{
  if (lambda >= 350 && lambda <= 439)
  {
    fRed    = -(lambda - (float)440.0) / ((float)440.0 - (float)350.0);
    fGreen = (float)0.0;
    fBlue      = (float)1.0;
  }
  else if (lambda >= (float)440.0 && lambda <= (float)489.0)
  {
    fRed        = 0.0;
    fGreen = (lambda - (float)440.0) / ((float)490.0 - (float)440.0);
    fBlue       = 1.0;
  }
  else if (lambda >= (float)490.0 && lambda <= (float)509.0)
```

```
    {
      fRed = 0.0;
      fGreen = 1.0;
      fBlue = -(lambda - (float)510.0) / ((float)510.0 - (float)490.0);

    }
    else if (lambda >= (float)510.0 && lambda <= (float)579.0)
    {
      fRed = (lambda - (float)510.0) / ((float)580.0 - (float)510.0);
      fGreen = 1.0;
      fBlue = 0.0;
    }
    else if (lambda >= (float)580.0 && lambda <= (float)644.0)
    {
      fRed = 1.0;
      fGreen = -(lambda - (float)645.0) / ((float)645.0 - (float)580.0);
      fBlue = 0.0;
    }
    else if (lambda >= 645.0 && lambda <= 780.0)
    {
      fRed = 1.0;
      fGreen = 0.0;
      fBlue = 0.0;
    }
    else
    {
      fRed = 0.0;
      fGreen = 0.0;
      fBlue = 0.0;
    }

    if (lambda >= 350 && lambda <= 419)
    {
        Factor = 0.3 + 0.7*(lambda - (float)350.0) / ((float)420.0 -
(float)350.0);
    }
    else if (lambda >= 420 && lambda <= 700)
    {
      Factor = 1.0;
    }
    else if (lambda >= 701 && lambda <= 780)
    {
        Factor = 0.3 + 0.7*((float)780.0 - lambda) / ((float)780.0 -
(float)700.0);
    }
    else
    {
      Factor = 0.0;
    }
    iR = factorAdjust(fRed, Factor, MaxIntensity, Gamma);
    iG = factorAdjust(fGreen, Factor, MaxIntensity, Gamma);
    iB = factorAdjust(fBlue, Factor, MaxIntensity, Gamma);
}

int factorAdjust(float C, float Factor, int MaxIntensity, float Gamma)
```

```
{
  if(C == 0.0)
  {
    return 0;
  }
  else
  {
    return (int) round(MaxIntensity * pow(C * Factor, Gamma));
  }
}
```

5. **Select an LED to test.** If you've purchased a large number of LEDs to test, they're likely to arrive in individual plastic pouches. Neatly pull or cut open the plastic pouch containing the LED, take the LED out, and set the pouch aside; you'll need it again soon (Figure 4-4).

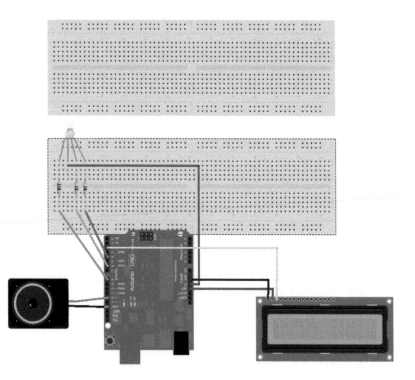

Figure 4-4. *Step four.*

6. **Connect the LED.** Hook up the anode to Arduino analog pin 0, and the cathode to GND (Figure 4-5).

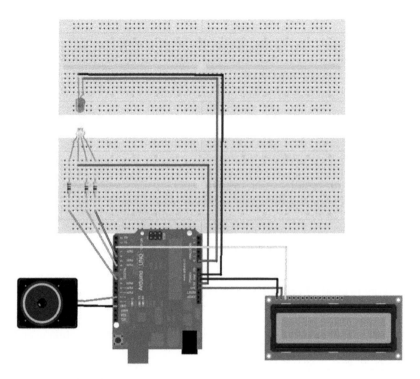

Figure 4-5. *Step five.*

 As you test each LED, be careful to plug it into the breadboard with the proper polarity: anode to Arduino's analog pin 0 and cathode to Ardunio's GND pin.

---

7. **Test the LED.** For best results, enclose the test LED and the RGB LED in a single small, opaque tube, such as a piece of shrinkwrap tubing, a blackened soda straw, or even the opaque, sawed-off body of a ball point pen. Ideally, the two LEDs should be extremly close without actually touching. When everything is ready, turn on or reset Arduino.

Several things will happen. The RGB LED will start to glow, and the top line of the LCD will inform you that the RGB LED is currently displaying a particular wavelength of light ranging from 350–700 nm. At each wavelength, the test LED absorbs the light being put out by the RGB LED, and converts that to a voltage.

- Low voltage means that the test LED is not absorbing much light at that wavelength; in other words, the test LED is not very sensitive to this color. A higher voltage indicates that the test LED is more sensitive to this particular wavelength and is therefore creating more electricity from the light it absorbs.
- As Arduino works its way up the spectrum, it keeps track of the peak voltage the test LED puts out, and the particular wavelength that caused the peak voltage.
- You'll know the test is complete when the counter reaches 700 nm, and Arduino plays a little melody.

8. **Note your results.** Using the permanent marker, write your data—the peak voltage and the light wavelength that caused it—on the plastic pouch that you set aside in step four. Carefully remove the test LED from the gadget and slide it back into the pouch.

9. Return to step five and hit the reset button on Arduino to repeat the sensitivity test with another LED.

In order to build an LED photometer that works properly, it's very important to test each LED before you use it in the photometer. You need to know the particular wavelengths of light that your LEDs are detecting, because this impacts the types of gases you'll be able to detect in the atmosphere, and how well you'll be able to detect them.

nm? What is this nm?

Wavelengths of light are so small they are measured not in millimeters (1/1,000ths of a meter) or micrometers (1/1,000,000ths of a meter) but in nanometers (1/1,000,000,000ths of a meter). Because wavelengths of light are so small, a great many things interfere with them. Imagine that you're inside a walk-in closet or windowless bathroom: by simply sealing the door, it would be easy to stop all light waves from entering the room. But if you had a portable radio with you (if you know what that is), or your cell phone (which is very much like a portable radio), you'd have no problem getting a radio signal even though all external light into your room was cut off—unless your closet was deep inside an underground, reinforced concrete security bunker!

Radio waves and light waves are the same physical phenomena: electromagnetic radiation, differing only in wavelength size. So we can say that clearly, light waves are more easily stopped by physical objects than other types of electromagnetic waves. In fact, that's the whole purpose of this LED photometer. Molecules of gas and particles of dust that by themselves are invisible to the naked eye all are large enough to interfere with certain wavelengths of light. By measuring which light waves are affected more strongly and which light waves are affected less strongly by the given particles in the atmosphere, we can get a very good estimate of the concentration of those gases or particles in the atmosphere.

Table 4-1 shows some values we got with a sample of LEDs from different manufacturers. Notice that while the LED peak input value is usually lower than the output value, that's not always the case. LEDs at the blue end of the spectrum have input wavelengths almost exactly the same as their output wavelengths. As we move down the spectrum toward the red end, the distance between input and oputput wavelength grows, but not uniformly. For example, look at the two yellow LEDs giving off light with a wavelength of 592 nm. Their input values are exactly 20 nm different!

This explains why we said earlier that it is important to test your LEDs. You need to know exactly which peak wavelength your LEDs are absorbing.

Table 4-1. *Frequencies of light for various LEDs by part number.*

Manufacturer	Mfgr Part Number	Color	Output nm	Input nm
Jameco Valuepro	LVB3330	Blue	430	429
Avago Technologies	QLMP-LB98	Blue	470	471
Avago Technologies	QLMP-LM98	Green	525	498
Agilent	HLMP-CM39-UVCDD	Green	535	505
Siemans Corporation	LG5469FH	Green	565	507
Valuepro	LUY3833H	Yellow	590	537
Valuepro	BVT-5E1TT4E	Yellow	592	552
Jameco Valuepro	BVT-529TT8E	Yellow	592	532
Valuepro	LVY3333/A	Yellow	595	532
Valuepro	RL50-PY543	Yellow	595	517
Valuepro	LUE3333	Orange	620	625
Valuepro	UT9C13-86-UDC2-R	Red	630	580
Jameco Valuepro	BVT-5E1QT4ER	Red	634	555
Valuepro	RL50-PR543	Red	635	534

5/Gadget: LED Photometer

A photometer is a device that measures one or more qualities of light. Most photometers consist of an interference filter and a photo detector. The interference filter is a colored piece of plastic or glass that filters out nonessential colors, letting through only the precise wavelengths of light we're interested in studying. A photo detector behind that filter monitors the intensity of the light that makes it through the filter.

In this gadget, LEDs replace both the interference filter and the photo detector. As Forrest Mims showed, LEDs are photodiodes: diodes that generate electrical current proportional to the light that falls on them, and they act as their own color filter. As you learned from your own experiments with the LED sensitivity tester, a blue LED is most sensitive to blue light and much less sensitive to red. By recording the amount of current from differently colored LEDs, we can learn how much of each color of the sun's light (blue, green, and red) is getting through the atmosphere to the gadget.

The main advantage of an LED photometer is that it is relatively inexpensive. LEDs are cheap, rugged, and stable. They come in a variety of colors and a variety of spectral responses. The electronics that go with them can be purchased online or at any good electronics store.

A couple things to keep in mind:

- Although LEDs can work as detectors, they were not built for this purpose. Whereas an ideal detector for our needs would detect only a very narrow range of wavelengths, and be perfectly centered around the wavelengths we wish to study, LEDs can detect light over a fairly wide range of wavelengths. That's why we've tested the LEDs: to know their detection peaks, so that we know which wavelengths of light we're measuring.

- Also, the current generated by an LED can change with the temperature of the LED; for this reason, we advise you to keep the gadget at room temperature, and make all outside measurements relatively quickly, before the gadget heats up (or cools down) too much.

Even allowing for these shortcomings, however, it is perfectly possible to get scientifically valid data by using the LED detectors to measure the upper atmosphere.

Build the Gadget

Amount	Part Type	Properties
1	Piezo Speaker	
1	Blue LED, 5 mm	Package 5 mm [THT]; leg yes; color Blue
1	Green LED, 5 mm	Package 5 mm [THT]; leg yes; color Green
1	Red LED, 5 mm	Package 5 mm [THT]; leg yes; color Red
1	Arduino	Processor ATmega; variant Arduino
1	LCD screen	Type character; pins 16

There are two sequences of steps that are equally essential to creating the LED photometer: building it, and calibrating it.

1. Connect the LEDs to Arduino (Figure 5-1). We've found it's easiest to do this as follows:

   a. Connect the negative (i.e., shorter wire) of each LED to the GND rail of the breadboard.

   b. Connect the positive (i.e., longer wire) of each LED to the breadboard.

   c. Using jumpers, connect each LED to the appropriate Analog pin on Arduino. Our Arduino sketch expects the red LED to be plugged into A1, the green LED into A2, and the blue LED into A3.

2. Connect the speaker (Figure 5-2). Plug the positive lead into Arduino digital pin 7 and the negative pin into Arduino GND. Many speakers don't list the polarity of their connection, so don't worry too much about this; just plug it in!

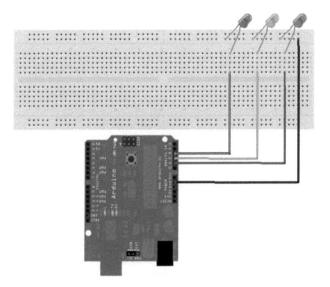

Figure 5-1. *Step one.*

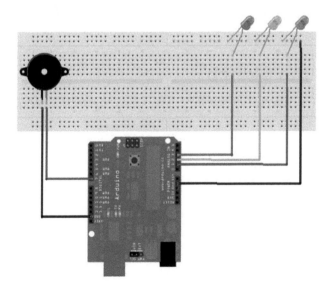

Figure 5-2. *Step two.*

3. Connect the LCD unit to Arduino (Figure 5-3). The data line connects to Arduino digital pin 5, the power line connects to Arduino 3.3 v pin, and GND line connects to GND.

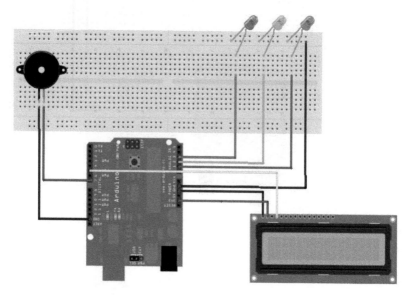

Figure 5-3. *Step three.*

Load the Sketch

You can find this sketch in the AMWA GitHub repository (*https://github.com/ejgertz/AMWA*).

```
/*
 LED Photometer, based on Analog Input
 by Patrick Di Justo
 2012 08 30
*/

#include <EEPROM.h>
#include <SD.h>
#include <SoftwareSerial.h>

// Liquid Crystal Display
// Define the LCD pins: We'll be using a serial-based LCD display
// which only required +3.3Volts, GND, and a single data line.
// databuff and displaybuff hold the data to be displayed

#define LCDIn  3
```

```
#define LCDOut 5
SoftwareSerial mySerialPort(LCDIn, LCDOut);

// Data Buffers for the LCD
char databuff1[16];
char databuff2[16];
char dispbuff[16];

// LED variables section
// Which Arduino pin goes to which LED
int redPin = A1;
int greenPin =A2;
int bluePin=A3;


// A place to store the values coming from the analog port
int sensorValueRed =0;
int sensorValueGreen =0;
int sensorValueBlue = 0;

//A place to store the maximum value for each LED
int maxRed = 0;
int maxGreen =0;
int maxBlue = 0;


//EEPROM variables
// The record length is 7: 1 byte for the record number, 2 bytes
// each for the 3 LEDs.  For each additional LED you add, increase
// the record length by 2.
int record=0;
int reclen = 7;
int addr =0;

// the following variable is long because the time, measured in
miliseconds,
// will quickly become a bigger number than can be stored in an int.
long timeSinceLastSensorHigh = 0;
int dataWritten = 0;

// music section
int notelen =40;
int dlx = notelen *1.33;

//switch to tell if an SD card is present
int SDPresent = 1;

void setup()
{
  // initialize serial communications at 9600 bps:
  Serial.begin(9600);

  // Set the Analog Pins
  // Why are we setting input pins to output?
  // We're doing this to prevent "leakage" from the pins.
```

```
  // Setting the pins to output activates a pullup resistor,
  // which makes it difficult for voltage to come into the Arduino,
  // until we're ready for it.

  Serial.println("Setting up the Analog Pins");

  pinMode(redPin, OUTPUT);
  digitalWrite(redPin, LOW);
  pinMode(greenPin, OUTPUT);
  digitalWrite(greenPin, LOW);
  pinMode(bluePin, OUTPUT);
  digitalWrite(bluePin, LOW);

  // Set up SD card, let us know if SD card is absent
  pinMode(10, OUTPUT);
  if (!SD.begin(4)) delay(10);
    SDPresent =0;

  //Set up LCD
  pinMode(LCDOut, OUTPUT);

  mySerialPort.begin(9600);
  mySerialPort.write(0xFE);
  mySerialPort.write(0x01);
  sprintf(databuff1,"Wakeup Test");
  sprintf(dispbuff,"%-16s",databuff1);
  mySerialPort.print(dispbuff);


//set up EEPROM
  record = EEPROM.read(0);
  addr = (record * reclen) +1;
  Serial.println("BEEP");

// Play music to let user know the gadget is ready
  tone(7,294,notelen);
  delay(dlx);
  tone(7,330,notelen);
  delay(dlx);
  tone(7,261,notelen);
  delay(dlx);
  tone(7,131,notelen);
  delay(dlx);
  tone(7,196,notelen);
  delay(dlx);
  delay(3000);
}


void loop()
{
  // read the value from the sensor:
  /*
    Back in setup(), we enabled a pullup resistor on the analog pins, which
    made it difficult for electricity to come into the analog pins.
```

Here, we disable the pullup resistor, wait 10ms for the pin to stabilize,
read the voltage coming into the pin, then reenable the pullup resistor.
*/

```
pinMode(redPin, INPUT);
delay(10);
Serial.print("Reading red:  ");
sensorValueRed= analogRead(redPin);
pinMode(redPin, OUTPUT);
Serial.println(sensorValueRed);
delay(10);

pinMode(greenPin, INPUT);
delay(10);
sensorValueGreen = analogRead(greenPin);
pinMode(greenPin, OUTPUT);
delay(10);

pinMode(bluePin, INPUT);
delay(10);
sensorValueBlue = analogRead(bluePin);
pinMode(bluePin, OUTPUT);
delay(10);

Serial.println("Comparing sensor values...");

// Here we compare each sensor to its maximum value.
// If any of the sensors has reached a new peak, sound a tone
if(   (sensorValueRed>maxRed)
   || (sensorValueGreen>maxGreen)
   || (sensorValueBlue>maxBlue))
  {
  tone(7,maxRed+maxGreen+maxBlue,500);
  timeSinceLastSensorHigh = millis();
  }

// Here we reset the old maximum value with a new one, if necessary
if(sensorValueRed>maxRed) maxRed = sensorValueRed;
if(sensorValueGreen>maxGreen) maxGreen = sensorValueGreen;
if(sensorValueBlue>maxBlue) maxBlue = sensorValueBlue;

// Display the sensor values on the LCD screen
sprintf(databuff1,"R%3d G%3d B%3d",maxRed,maxGreen,maxBlue);
sprintf(dispbuff,"%-16s",databuff1);
mySerialPort.print(dispbuff);
Serial.print(dispbuff);
```

// If 10 seconds has gone by without any new measurements, write
// data to storage.

```
if(millis() > (timeSinceLastSensorHigh + 10000))
   {
   if(dataWritten ==0)
```

```
      {
        writeData();
        if(SDPresent = 1)
          {
          writeDataToSD(databuff1, databuff2);
          }
        }
      }
}


void writeData()
{
  Serial.print("I'm writing data!!!!!!!!!!!!!!!!!");
  record++;
  EEPROM.write(0, record);
  EEPROM.write(addr++, record);

  /*
  The problems of data storage:
   The analog pins read a value from 0 to 1023. This is 1024 different
values,
   and 1024 = 2 ^ 10. It would take 10 bits of data space to safely
   store the value from the analog pins.  Unfortunately, a standard byte
   of data is only 8 bits.  How can you fit 10 bits into 8 bits?
   You can't.

   What we're doing here is splitting the 10 bits of data into two sections,
   which can be stored in two bytes of memory space.
  */

  int quotient = sensorValueRed/256;
  int mod = sensorValueRed % 256;
  EEPROM.write(addr++,quotient);
  EEPROM.write(addr++,mod);

  quotient = sensorValueGreen/256;
  mod = sensorValueGreen % 256;
  EEPROM.write(addr++,quotient);
  EEPROM.write(addr++,mod);

  quotient = sensorValueBlue/256;
  mod = sensorValueBlue % 256;
  EEPROM.write(addr++,quotient);
  EEPROM.write(addr++,mod);
  dataWritten = 1;

  sprintf(databuff1,"EEPROM written");
  sprintf(dispbuff,"%-16s",databuff1);
  mySerialPort.print(dispbuff);
  Serial.println("FINAL BEEP");

  tone(7,196,notelen);
```

```
  delay(dlx);

  tone(7,131,notelen);
  delay(dlx);

  tone(7,261,notelen);
  delay(dlx);

  tone(7,330,notelen);
  delay(dlx);

  tone(7,294,notelen);
}


void writeDataToSD(String dataString1, String dataString2)
{
  // open the file. note that only one file can be open at a time,
  // so you have to close this one before opening another.
  File dataFile = SD.open("LEDdata.txt", FILE_WRITE);

  // if the file is available, write to it:
  if (dataFile)
  {
    dataFile.print(millis());
    dataFile.print(",");
    dataFile.println(dataString1);
    dataFile.close();

    sprintf(databuff1,"SDCard written");
    sprintf(dispbuff,"%-16s",databuff1);
    mySerialPort.print(dispbuff);
  }
}
```

Calibrate the Gadget: Air Mass, Atmospheric Optical Thickness, and Extraterrestrial Constant

Remember when we said that the sunlight travels to the ground through different thickness of atmosphere, depending on how high the sun is above the horizon? This can have an effect on the readings you get with your LED photometer, as well (see Figure 5-4).

Figure 5-4. *Sun angles in spring, summer, fall, and winter.*

Generally, this device is meant to measure the atmosphere at around noon each day, when the sun is at its highest in the sky and its path through the atmosphere is shortest. At the very least, if you can't make regular noon measurements, you should try to take measurements around the same time each day.

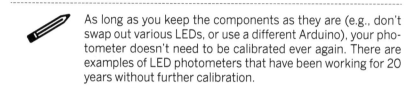

As long as you keep the components as they are (e.g., don't swap out various LEDs, or use a different Arduino), your photometer doesn't need to be calibrated ever again. There are examples of LED photometers that have been working for 20 years without further calibration.

But that raises an interesting problem: as the Earth revolves around the sun, the position of the sun at noon changes enormously over the course of the year. On the first day of summer, the noonday sun is as close to being directly overhead as it will ever get, while on the first day of winter, the noonday sun hugs the horizon 47° lower than the summer sun. This can have a profound effect on the measurements you get with your LED photometer, since the sunlight is moving through significantly differing distances of air through the course of a year.

This is why we have to take into account a value called *air mass*. The formula for air mass is very simple:

$m = 1 / sin(theta)$

where theta is the angle of the sun above the horizon.

Let's take a look at how the air mass at noon will differ over the course of a year from A.M.W.A. World Headquarters (see Table 5-1).

Table 5-1. *Sun angles and air mass from New York City.*

Date	Noon Sun Angle	Air Mass
March 20, 2013	49.4	1.3170
June 21, 2013	72.7	1.0474
September 22, 2013	49.3	1.3190
December 21, 2013	25.9	2.2894

At noon on the first day of spring, March 20, the noon sun is 49.4° above the horizon. Plugging that into the preceding formula results in an air mass of about 1.3170. This means that the sun's light had to travel through 1.3170 times as much air as it would if the sun were directly overhead.

At midday on the first day of summer, June 21, the sun was at 72.7° above the horizon. This gives us an air mass of 1.0474, meaning that the sun's light had to travel through 1.0474 times as much air as it would if the sun were directly overhead; that's a pretty negligible difference on its own terms, but about 25% lower than the air mass in March.

On September 22, the first day of autumn, the sun returned to 49.3° above the horizon, almost exactly where it was in March.

On December 21, the first day of winter, the sun at noon was 25.9° above the horizon. Plugging that into the preceding formula, we see that the air mass is a whopping 2.2895! The sun's light is traveling through more than twice as much air as it did on the first day of summer. This is an enormous difference, and, if uncorrected, would have an effect on the data we collect.

To fix this, we can use the data we collect to calculate a value called the *atmospheric optical thickness* (AOT). AOT measures the clarity of the air for any given air mass by comparing the data that you measure on the surface of the earth with the data your LED photometer would get if it were above the atmosphere, out in space.

Are we going to send our LED photometer into space? If only! Although that sounds like a great project, it's a little beyond the scope of this book—and unnecessary. What we're going to do is to take several measurements that will tell us what our LED photometer would measure *if it were out in space*.

Calculating Atmospheric Optical Thickness

Once you've built your LED photometer, wait for an exceptionally clear day. You'll want a day where the humidity remains constant, the cloud cover is almost nonexistent, and a place where there are no obvious nearby forest fires, or anything else that would contribute haze to the atmosphere. (Conversely, you could also wait for an overcast day, as long as the cloud cover is uniform. However, the data you get might not be as good as one from an exceptionally clear day.)

On this clear day, you're going to take a series of measurements with your LED photometer every half hour for half of the daylight hours (Table 5-2). You can take these measurements from dawn until noon, or from noon until sunset. Carefully keep track of the sun's angle above the horizon at each measurement point.

Table 5-2. *Solar data, noon to near sunset.*

Time	Sun Angle	Air Mass	Averaged LED Value
12:00	58	1.179	578.33
12:30	57.2	1.189	539
13:00	55	1.220	553

13:30	51.8	1.272	552
14:00	47.9	1.347	563.33
14:30	43.3	1.458	552.66
15:00	38.3	1.613	575
15:30	33	1.836	520.33
16:00	27.5	2.165	539
16:30	21.9	2.681	502
17:00	16.3	3.562	490
17:10	14.4	4.021	474.66
17:20	12.5	4.620	472.66
17:30	10.6	5.436	463.33
17:40	8.7	6.611	443.33

 To find the angle of the sun at any given time of day, visit the US Naval Observatory's Sun Calculator (*http:// aa.usno.navy.mil/data/docs/AltAz.php*).

Once you've collected this data, take it back to your workstation and, using graph paper or a spreadsheet program, create a scatter chart in which the Y axis is the logarithm of the data from any one of the LEDs (or all of the LEDs) and the X axis is the air mass at which these readings were taken.

Draw a best-fit line through the data points you get, and extend that line back to the Y intercept where the air mass is zero. The Y value at that point is known as the *extraterrestrial constant*, or EC. (If you're using a spreadsheet, look for a function called linear regression to accomplish the same thing.) Once you've calculated the EC, your LED photometer is calibrated.

Now that we've derived EC, we can finally use that to calculate atmospheric optical thickness, using the following formula:

AOT = (log(EC) / log(LED photometer reading)) / m

When your data is run through this formula, it will be scientifically "fit." The natural variance in the height of the sun above the horizon at various times of year is now accounted for. The AOT is the true measure of atmospheric optical thickness and should apply to all data you collect with your LED photometer.

Things to Try

Now that you've built the apparatus, let's look at some things that you can do with it.

Detecting "Ozone Holes": Measuring the Ozone Layer

The ozone layer is a narrow band in the Earth's atmosphere, approximately 25 kilometers above the surface, where the concentration of the O_3 ozone molecule is relatively high, reaching about 10 parts per million (compared to the usual 0.6 ppm in other parts of the atmosphere).

The ozone layer is essential to life on Earth, because it absorbs around 97% of the ultraviolet radiation from the sun, in the range of about 200–315 nm (what scientists and sunscreen manufacturers call the UV-B band). UV-B rays have enough energy to damage many biological molecules, including DNA. Without an ozone layer, the Earth might never have developed life.

Save the Ozone Layer!

Widespread use of molecules called chlorofluorocarbons (CFCs) as propellants in aerosol cans did a significant amount of damage to the ozone layer in the 20th century; CFCs can break apart ozone molecules, leaving them unable to absorb UV light. A 1987 international agreement, called the Montreal Protocol on Substances that Deplete the Ozone Layer (or just "Montreal Protocol" for short), banned most CFCs from use; nearly 200 nations have ratified it. Still, CFC residues remain in the stratosphere; some studies report a 4% decrease in ozone concentrations per decade since the late 20th century. However, since the turn of the century, scientists have begun to detect evidence of ozone layer recovery, as well.

Measuring the ozone layer with LEDs is conceptually not very difficult: all you'd need to do is to find an LED that aborbs ultraviolet light in the UV-A range (about 200–315 nm), and compare its output with an LED that absorbs light in the UV-B range. If the ozone layer didn't exist, the surface measurement of UV-A and UV-B would be equal, so any difference in the reading of the two LEDs would most likely be related to the presence of the ozone layer.

All this seems easy enough to allow you to build an upper atmosphere ozone monitor; but as a practical matter, UV LEDS become more and more expensive as you go down the wavelengths. It's also considerably more difficult (and requires more and different equiment) to test a UV LED to see its absorption range.

However, there might be another way to make this work. Everyone knows that ozone absorbs ultraviolet light, but not many people know that ozone also has an absorption band centered around 602 nm, in the orange part of the spectrum. This region, called the Chappuis band, is nowhere near as deep as the UV-B absorption bands; still, scientists have gotten good data from measuring how ozone absorbs orange light. Perhaps you can build an LED photometer that measures the ozone absorption in the orange part of the spectrum, if you can find an LED sensitive to 602 nm. Good luck!

Add an Accelerometer

Adding an accelerometer to the LED photometer will automatically tell you the angle at which you're pointing the device at the sun.

As we noted earlier, the sun's angle at noon can vary by 47° over the course of a year. While it's not going to kill you to expend the effort to look up or calculate the sun's declination when you take a measurement, it would be infinitely easier if Arduino itself told you the angle. You can make this happen with a multiple axis accelerometer attached to your Arduino. This can make the calculation of AOT so simple you might be able to include it in the Arduino code, and store the resulting value with the rest of the data.

But there's a drawback: most accelerometers use up to three analog inut pins to get data to Arduino. You might have to cut back on the number of LEDs you're using, if you use an accelerometer. If you can think of another way to make this work, we'd love to hear from you.

6/Using the LED Photometer

One of the oldest bits of weather lore is "Red sky at night, sailor's delight. Red sky in morning, sailors take warning." The sky is often red, or reddish orange, at sunrise and sunset. Reds, pinks, and oranges dominate at these times of day because the distance from your eye to the sun is greater at these times than when the sun is directly overhead. When sunlight travels through the atmosphere—and especially when it travels that extra distance from the horizon—an effect known as *Rayleigh scattering* takes place.

The British physicist John William Strutt (the third Baron Rayleigh) explained in 1871 that air molecules are so small they interfere with and scatter photons of light. The various molecules that make up the Earth's natural atmosphere —mostly nitrogen and oxygen, with trace amounts of other gases—scatter blue light (shorter wavelength light) more efficiently than red, orange, or yellow light (longer wavelengths). So when you look up, you see more scattered blue light than red or orange light. This is why our sky appears blue during most of the daytime (Figure 6-1).

When the sun is on the horizon at dawn or dusk, however, its light must travel through more of the atmosphere before we see it than when it is overhead (Figure 6-2). This leads to more and more of the blue light being scattered away, leaving behind the red-orange-yellow light. As well, dust and aerosols in the atmosphere more ably scatter long wavelengths of light—leading to lurid red sunsets.

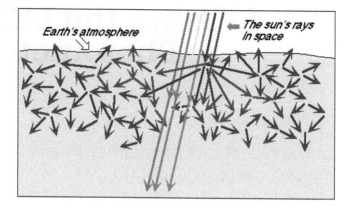

Figure 6-1. *As sunlight hits the Earth's atmosphere, air molecules scatter the shorter, blue wavelengths of light, but let the longer wavelengths through. Credit: NOAA ERSL (http://www.esrl.noaa.gov/gmd/grad/about/ redsky/index.html).*

As atmospheric particles get larger, they tend to scatter all wavelengths of light equally and indiscriminately. This explains why clouds, which are made of relatively large water droplets, are white.

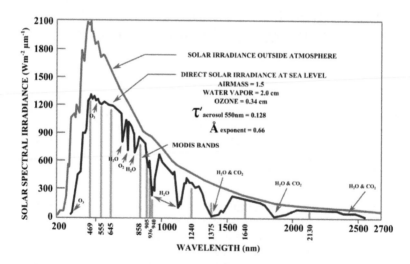

Figure 6-2. *This chart describes the absorption of sunlight by various atmospheric molecules. Look carefully in the 700 nm range of wavelengths: the dips in the "Direct Solar Irradiance at Sea Level" line indicate where molecules like water and oxygen are blocking out certain wavelengths of sunlight.*

Of course, molecules don't just scatter wavelengths of light. Certain molecules, such as water vapor, carbon dioxide, and ozone, also absorb specific wavelengths of light. To a measuring instrument on the ground, there is less light at those specific wavelengths than there is at other nearby wavelengths, because some of that light has been absorbed. By measuring these "holes" where wavelengths of light are absent, you can get a very good estimate of how much water vapor, ozone, and some other substances are in the atmosphere above your head.

Atmospheric Aerosols

Atmospheric aerosols are tiny particles of matter suspended in the atmosphere. These minute particles scatter and absorb sunlight, reducing the clarity and color of what we see. This is the effect we're referring to when we talk about "haze" in the sky.

Sources of Haze

Atmospheric haze comes from diverse sources. Most inhabited places on Earth always have some water vapor in the atmosphere, and enough water vapor can cause haze. Clouds and fog add more particles to the atmosphere, making visibility even hazier. Forest fires, volcanic eruptions, and dust storms can all increase haze in the atmosphere, sometimes hundreds of miles away from where they originate.

Human activites contribute to haze as well: smoke given off by cooking or heating fires, for example, or by industrial facilities such as coal-fired power plants. When sunlight hits the exhaust from automotive vehicles, the nitrogen oxides and hydrocarbons in the exhaust react to create photochemical smog and ozone; both create haze. Even contrails from high flying airplanes can make the sky hazy.

According to the US Environmental Protection Agency, since 1988 the atmosphere in national parks and wilderness areas in the United States has gotten so hazy that average visibility has dropped from 90 miles to 15–25 miles in the east, and from 140 miles to 35–90 miles in the west.

The LED photometer measures the difference between the voltage produced by a red LED, which absorbs light around the 580 nm range, and the voltage produced by a green LED, which absorbs light around the 500 nm range. The readings appear on the LCD, and are then stored on the Arduino's EEPROM (and/or SD card, if you choose to use one).

You can chart this data by hand, extract the data, and graph it in a spreadsheet program, or upload it to Cosm (*http://www.cosm.com*) (formerly Pachube) to share it with the world. More on this shortly.

On a clear day with very little haze, the voltages produced by the green LED and red LED will be somewhat similar. As atmospheric aerosols increase, however—whether over the course of a day, several days, or from season to season—the difference between the red LED's voltage and the green LED's voltage will increase. The green LED will produce less current when there is more atmospheric haze, because less green light than usual is reaching it.

The voltages will almost never be exactly the same; Rayleigh scattering guarantees that more green light will be scattered by our atmosphere than red light. Also, white light reflected by clouds can sometimes cause the green LED to spike. The best results come from days without clouds (or with a uniform cloud cover).

Photosynthetically Active Radiation (PAR)

Photosynthesis, the process by which green plants turn sunlight into carbohydrates, does not use green light.

Plants appear green precisely because they *reflect* green light; they have no use for those wavelengths, and therefore can afford to throw them away. Green leaves absorb a great deal of the light at red and blue wavelengths. You can use LEDs to measure how much of those wavelengths—how much photosynthetically active radiation—is reaching your detector.

You do this by summing the outputs from two LEDs: the same red LED as in the aerosol detector, and a blue LED. As with the aerosol detector, Arduino reads the voltages produced by the red and blue LEDs, displays them, and stores them where they can be graphed, extracted into a spreadsheet, or uploaded to Cosm.

Forrest M. Mims, the man who discovered the Mims effect, has shown that using red and blue LEDs to measure photosynthetically active radiation agrees very well with more "professional" PAR sensors.

Water Vapor (WV)

Atmospheric water vapor absorbs EM wavelengths in the range of infrared light, at around 940 nm. By using an infrared LED specifically designed to absorb light at 940 nm, you can get a very accurate representation of the amount of water vapor in the atmosphere. Simply compare the outputs of the 940 nm LED with a similar infrared LED sensitive to around 880 nm.

One thing to keep in mind, however, is that this type of measurement is incredibly dependent upon local weather conditions. The rapid passage of a storm front over your observational area can play havoc with your readings: obviously there's going to be more water vapor in the air when it is raining, snowing, or about to do either. Thus, this gadget is better suited to measuring upper atmosphere water vapor—water vapor high above what we might think of as "the weather." Because of this, the best water vapor measurements are those made on clear days.

Extracting Data from the LED Photometer

Okay, so you've collected a bunch of data with your LED photometer. What do you do now?

Graphing Data in a Spreadsheet

Once you've processed the data in a spreadsheet, you can graph it. Your results might end up looking like these charts by Forrest M. Mims, who has been collecting atmospheric data with an LED photometer in Texas since the early 1990s (Figure 6-3).

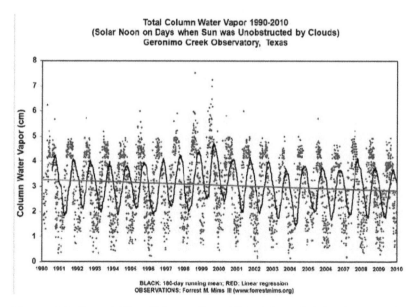

Figure 6-3. *Forrest Mims III has gathered this data on total water vapor in the atmosphere using an LED-based photometer. Image used with permission.*

Notice the patterns in Mims's decades of data: nearly every reading shows some kind of seasonal variation. It might take a year or more before you can see a full cycle in your data.

Sending Data to COSM

You can upload your data for all the Internet to see thanks to a service called Cosm (*http://www.cosm.com*). Our previous book, *Environmental Monitoring With Arduino* (*http://shop.oreilly.com/product/0636920021582.do*) (O'Reilly), contains a whole tutorial on getting started with Cosm; for now, let's just say that Cosm makes it very easy to upload a CSV data file. Just cut and paste the serial output of the EEPROM reader program, or use the file *DATALOG.TXT* from the SD card, and place it on your website. Then go to your Cosm account and tell it where to find that file. Before you know it, your LED photometer data will be on the internet, neatly graphed, for all the world to see.

7/Doing Science: How to Learn More from Your Atmospheric Data

Science can be defined as the practice of observing the natural world, and trying to make objective sense of it by uncovering facts or cause-and-effect relationships.

The gadgets in this book detect substances and conditions in the atmosphere that otherwise would be invisible to your senses. (Essentially, the gadgets are technological extensions of your senses.) Building them will help hone your skills with DIY electronics and Arduino programming. These are fun, interesting, and practical things to do—but doing them by themselves is not doing science.

Suppose you'd like to learn more from what you uncover. Maybe you'd like to measure atmospheric conditions over days or weeks, and then interpret those readings; or monitor the atmosphere in different parts of your neighborhood, county, or state, and compare that data usefully; or perhaps even organize people around the world to build gas sensors or photometers, and compare findings from these different places in meaningful ways. To do these things, you'll need to apply some intellectual elbow grease to how you use your gadget. You'll have to do some science.

The Scientific Method

The scientific method is the foundation of how most of the serious science in the world gets done. It's a systematic process of investigation that tests ideas about how cause and effect operate in the natural world, helps to reduce or eliminate bias, and allows the meaningful comparison of information from different sources.

The scientific method is appealingly linear in the abstract: an observation leads to a question, which leads to a hypothesis, which leads to an experiment, which leads to a result, which (if you're lucky) can lead to another question, and so the process begins again.

Testing hypotheses by gathering evidence is a core concern of science. What most scientists will tell you, though, is that their work tends not to progress as tidily as the scientific method looks on paper. More often they move back and forth between these steps, because science is an *iterative process*: a repeating process in which the end result is used as a starting point for the next run. Researchers often repeat the same steps over and over in order to test new ideas and tools, to deepen their questions about what they're studying, and to figure out how to do their research more effectively and accurately.

Researchers also test each other's hypotheses, because modern science demands that a result be *replicable*: that different people conducting identical experiments can come up with very similar, even identical results. If an experiment's results cannot be duplicated independently of the original researcher or team, then those results are cast into doubt.

Still, the scientific method is featured in the early chapters of many a Science 101 textbook because it's a good jumping-off point for learning how to set up an experiment and collect data.

Steps in the Scientific Method

At their most basic, the steps in the scientific method go like this:

- Observe something in the world.
- Ask a question about it.
- Formulate a potential answer (a hypothesis) for it.
- Conduct an experiment that tests the hypothesis.
- Compare the predicted result to the actual result:
  - Result supports the hypothesis.
  - Result doesn't support the hypothesis.
  - Result partially supports the hypothesis.
- Consider the result.
- Ask another question and begin again.

Let's look more closely at each step.

Observe Something in the World

Observation and exploration of what's going on in the environment is essential to figuring out what questions to ask. *Asking a question* really means "asking an answerable question," one that you can then test with an experiment. Testable questions begin with how, what, when, who, or which ("why" is impossible to answer).

Ask an Answerable Question

Devising a good experiment question can itself involve several steps. Is your question uninteresting or interesting? Can it be narrowed down to look at a single thing, to collect data on one variable only (an observational question), or to change one variable and learn what results (a manipulative question)? It's important to test only one variable—a factor that exists at different levels or amounts—at a time in your experiment, in order to be reasonably sure your test and the conclusions you draw from it are valid. If you test more than one variable at a time, then cause and effect relationships are much less clear.

An example of a testable question that would work with one of the gadgets in this book is, "When are atmospheric hydrocarbon levels outside my window at their highest concentration?"

Formulate a Hypothesis

Formulating a hypothesis involves using what you already know to come up with a potential answer to your question: an explanation for what you've observed. It's not merely an educated guess; it is your formal statement of what you're going to test (the variable) and a prediction of what the results will be.

For example, working off the previous question, you could form your hypothesis statement as, "If heavier car traffic increases atmospheric hydrocarbons outside my window, and I measure those levels from 4 to 6 pm as well as from 4 to 6 am, then I should detect higher levels from 4 to 6 pm, which is afternoon rush hour." The IF statement is your hypothesis; the AND statement is the design of your experiment; the THEN statement is your prediction of what you'll learn from the experiment. Since what you're measuring will be atmospheric hydrocarbons, the variable in this experiment is time.

Compare the Predicted to Actual Results, Considering the Results

On the face of it, this experiment sounds like a no-brainer: rush hour traffic means more car exhaust means higher levels of hydrocarbons, right? If your results support your hypothesis, then this experiment may be over.

But what if levels are low during both time periods? Those results fail to support your hypothesis. It wouldn't hurt to check your build and programming, to be sure the gadget is working correctly. Assuming it is, you may need to ask a new question, or broaden the scope of your experiment—such as taking measurements more often during the day, or on different days of the week, or during different types of weather.

And what if you get high hydrocarbon levels from 4 to 6 pm, and also from 4 to 6 am? That's a partial confirmation of your hypothesis that may lead you to...

Ask Another Question

Maybe there's something going on in the world around you that you didn't know about, like a delivery truck idling on the street early in the morning (we get that a lot on our street!). Do deliveries happen often enough to affect hydrocarbon levels most of the time, or just some of the time? To learn more, you'll need to figure out the next interesting, testable question, reformulate your hypothesis, and restructure your experiment.

By testing enough variables (time of day, day of week, month, weather conditions, etc.) you should be able to build up a very accurate profile of the hydrocarbon pollution outside your window. In fact, you should be able to predict future events: for example, if tomorrow is a delivery day, you could confidently predict there will be more pollution than usual. Or if tomorrow is going to be rainy, there will be less pollution, as the raindrops wash the pollution out of the atmosphere.

When you feel you've gotten the pollution profile for your neighborhood down pat, your work has just begun—now it's time to measure a different neighborhood! Science never stops!

About the Authors

Patrick Di Justo is a contributor to *Wired* magazine—where he writes the magazine's monthly "What's Inside" column—and the author of *The Science of Battlestar Galactica* (Wiley, October 2010). His work has appeared in *Dwell*, *Scientific American*, *Popular Science*, *The New York Times*, and more. He has also worked as a robot programmer for the Federal Reserve. He bought his first Arduino in 2007.

Emily Gertz has been covering DIY environmental monitoring since 2004, when she interviewed engineer-artist Natalie Jeremijenko for Worldchanging.com. Her work has also appeared in *Popular Science*, *Popular Mechanics*, *Scientific American*, *Grist*, *Dwell*, *OnEarth*, and more. She has been hands-on with Internet technologies since 1994 as a web producer, community host, and content and social media strategist.

Built with Atlas. O'Reilly Media, Inc., 2013.

Have it your way.

Get even more for your money.

Join the O'Reilly Community, and register the O'Reilly books you own. It's free, and you'll get:

- $4.99 ebook upgrade offer
- 40% upgrade offer on O'Reilly print books
- Membership discounts on books and events
- Free lifetime updates to ebooks and videos
- Multiple ebook formats, DRM FREE
- Participation in the O'Reilly community
- Newsletters
- Account management
- 100% Satisfaction Guarantee

Signing up is easy:

1. Go to: oreilly.com/go/register
2. Create an O'Reilly login.
3. Provide your address.
4. Register your books.

Note: English-language books only

To order books online:

oreilly.com/store

For questions about products or an order:

orders@oreilly.com

To sign up to get topic-specific email announcements and/or news about upcoming books, conferences, special offers, and new technologies:

elists@oreilly.com

For technical questions about book content:

booktech@oreilly.com

To submit new book proposals to our editors:

proposals@oreilly.com

O'Reilly books are available in multiple DRM-free ebook formats. For more information:

oreilly.com/ebooks